# Stoicism

Introduction to Applying the Ancient Philosophies of Stoicism

*(Complete Beginner's Guide to the Stoicism Way of Life)*

**Clarence Chacon**

Published By **Ryan Princeton**

## Clarence Chacon

All Rights Reserved

*Stoicism: Introduction to Applying the Ancient Philosophies of Stoicism (Complete Beginner's Guide to the Stoicism Way of Life)*

## ISBN 978-1-7388580-1-9

No part of this guidebook shall be reproduced in any form without permission in writing from the publisher except in the case of brief quotations embodied in critical articles or reviews.

Legal & Disclaimer

The information contained in this book is not designed to replace or take the place of any form of medicine or professional medical advice. The information in this book has been provided for educational & entertainment purposes only.

The information contained in this book has been compiled from sources deemed reliable, and it is accurate to the best of the Author's knowledge; however, the Author cannot guarantee its accuracy and validity and cannot be held liable for any errors or omissions. Changes are periodically made to this book. You must consult your doctor or get professional medical advice before using any of the suggested remedies, techniques, or information in this book.

Upon using the information contained in this book, you agree to hold harmless the Author from and against any damages, costs, and expenses, including any legal fees potentially resulting from the application of any of the information provided by this guide. This disclaimer applies to any damages or injury caused by the use and application, whether directly or indirectly, of any advice or information presented, whether for breach of contract, tort, negligence, personal injury, criminal intent, or under any other cause of action.

You agree to accept all risks of using the information presented inside this book. You need to consult a professional medical practitioner in order to ensure you are both able and healthy enough to participate in this program.

Table Of Contents

Chapter 1: Stoicism – What is it and Where Did it Come From? ................................. 1

Chapter 2: Expectations and Demands – Dealing with Modern Day Life ................ 13

Chapter 3: Seneca – Dealing With Stressful Situations ............................................... 22

Chapter 4: Problem Solving/Perseverance/Pragmatism Techniques .............................................. 32

Chapter 5: Daily Stoic Meditations and Affirmations ........................................... 45

Chapter 6 : Other Day-to-Day Stoic Tips of a Spy ..................................................... 57

Chapter 7: The Tragedy That Gave Birth to Stoicism ................................................. 65

Chapter 8: Virtues of Stoicism ................ 83

Chapter 9: Justice and Courage .............. 98

Chapter 10: The Three Disciplines of Stoicism ............................................... 114

Chapter 11: Applying Stoicism in Your Daily Life ...................................................... 137

Chapter 12: Living the Life of a Stoic .... 146

Chapter 13: What is Stoicism? A Brief History ................................................. 180

# Chapter 1: Stoicism – What is it and Where Did it Come From?

"A Stoic is a person who transforms fear into prudence, ache into transformation, errors into initiation, and desire into challenge"

(Nassim Taleb)

Stoicism in essence, is a easy philosophy which can assist make you a happier and more awesome individual. Although its roots date again to Ancient Greece, it has considering positioned a receptive target market in the 21st century. There are many these days who actively try and workout its tenets and characteristic even prepared themselves into online corporations who are supporting each others efforts. Holding digital sports which encompass Stoic Week, which disturbing conditions human beings to stay as Stoics for seven days.

However the bulk of human beings even though do no longer completely understand just what Stoicism is. If you had been to ask them what precisely they receive as actual with being a Stoic includes, they will say such things as "the potential to cover emotion, even while you're in ache, or gift technique some high-quality adverse or immoderate feeling." Although keeping feelings under control is an vital characteristic of a Stoic mentality, it isn't the first-class factor which defines Stoicism.

What is Stoicism?

So what exactly does the principle of Stoicism embody? It is a university of idea which have become based totally totally and advanced round 301 BC through manner of Zeno of Citium. Its name comes from the stoa poikile or painted porch, from which instructors lectured to university college college students. Stoicism emerged following the loss of life of Alexander the Great in 323 BC, which resulted in the breakup of his high-quality empire, and a duration of political turmoil wherein multiple activities were competing for electricity.

Stoicism aided its enthusiasts in managing the social uncertainty of this era, and therefore, quick obtained many adherents who helped to increase its tenets by means of using way of utilising them to their regular lives. There were 3 tremendous thinkers during this period who are seen as vital in the development of Stoicisms number one tenets:

Marcus Aurelius (121 AD to 180 AD) ruled as Emperor of Rome from 161 AD to one hundred and eighty AD. He changed into the writer of the e-book Meditations, a personal diary in which he chronicled his warfare to stay as much as Stoic ideals and necessities inside the route of the most hard days of his reign.

Epictetus (55 AD to a hundred thirty five AD) have become a former slave who have end up a teacher of philosophy after he come to be freed. His Handbook and four volumes of the Discourses are among the foundational texts of Stoicism, and were compiled with the useful resource of a former student thru his lectures after his loss of life.

Seneca (four BC to sixty 5 AD) have turn out to be a statesman who have become a train and adviser to the Emperor Nero, however who also wrote substantially approximately Stoicism and philosophy. His most prominent works regarding Stoicism are in the form of letters which he wrote to his friends, and which is probably amassed in books which incorporates Letters from a Stoic and On the Brevity of Life.

An important element to endure in mind is that first-class a very small percent of what the unique Stoic instructors wrote survives in recent times and for this reason, a number of what is taught as Stoicism is primarily based on the interpretation of students, and other practitioners of these fragments. However, there may be today's settlement that the subsequent constitute the clean principles of Stoicism:

Virtue

Virtue is defined as conduct which presentations excessive ethical requirements, which highlights the concept that Stoicism is a philosophy that is to be placed into exercise, in preference to clearly being favored intellectually as precis ideas (the chapters inside the latter a part of this e-book will assist you try this). Stoics bear in thoughts there to be four center virtues:

• Wisdom. This is a distinctive feature which may be tough to define, but is typically understood as being the identifying problem on how we need to behave in ultra-modern. How we ought to act and assume in the proper way thru integrating experience and records. For the Stoics, the maximum crucial shape of interest is the issues of ethical thinking (having the potential to differentiate proper from wrong) and practicality (being capable of make the right selections in keeping with this).

- Justice. This awesome characteristic refers to our capability to deal with others quite and with even-handedness, however additionally with kindness.

- Courage. For Stoics, this exclusive characteristic encourages a willingness to stand and master ones fears. This is especially relevant nearly approximately private improvement and existence selections.

- Temperance. Better known as moderation, is the virtue which pertains to being able to manipulate ones dreams.

To the Ancient Stoics, cultivating specific feature modified into often seemed due to the fact the most essential thing a person need to do. When we stay according with virtue, we are not quality living in concord with one-of-a-kind humans, however moreover with our simple nature as rational creatures, and with nature as a whole. In practical terms, this means we're able to face each difficult people, and bodily adversity with staying strength, degree-headedness and specific grace.

For Stoics, exceptional function offers us with the technique to show into our quality selves. In reality, they believed the very last purpose of human striving is to advantage eudaimonia, a Greek word which loosely translates into "happiness/well-being" or "human flourishing". For Stoics, this really intended residing in concord with nature.

Emotions

One of the most crucial misconceptions concerning Stoicism, which I even have already noted, is that practitioners of the philosophy do no longer display emotion. However, Stoics simply recollect the opportunity. They posit that someone in reality need to reveal emotion, however divide the ones feelings into "suitable" and "terrible". Bad or poor feelings, together with worry and anger, are those which might be based totally totally on faulty judgments, inclusive of even as we take outside activities too severely.

On the alternative hand, healthy and fine feelings are the result of creating practical judgments. According to the Stoics, there are 3 preferred commands of favorable feelings:

- Joy or pleasure, which takes satisfaction in what's really remarkable (such as extremely good human fulfillment) in preference to regards to extra superficial subjects.

- Discretion or warning, that's directed in the course of the factors of existence which can be definitely risky to us, on the facet of vice and folly.

- Willing what is absolutely accurate, inclusive of wishing the tremendous for others and ourselves, in vicinity of craving for matters which might be beyond our control, which incorporates indiscriminate wealth and unique peoples perception people.

For Ancient Stoics, the last goal come to be not to be emotionally disadvantaged, or to end up a person with a coronary heart of stone. But as an opportunity to domesticate self-love in addition to a right task for others, however continuously tempered by using know-how. For example, we are capable to reveal our love for others with the resource of working closer to philanthropy.

Of path, there are great involuntary emotional reactions which we experience in incredible conditions, collectively with being startled or embarrassed. However we need to now not allow the ones limbic tool, reflex-like expressions to turn into complete-blown emotional suggests. Instead we have to pick out the way to reply to the scenario logically, and after sound attention.

Nature and Humankind

As I honestly have already mentioned, one of the maximum essential goals of training Stoicism have become to stay in agreement with nature. For Stoics, there had been three components to this:

1.   Our internal nature, which represents our capability for cause.

2.   The nature of society and the manner we have interaction with the relaxation of humankind.

three.         The nature of the outside environment round us.

Thus, Stoics recommended us to appearance ourselves as a part of nature and of a more entire. By now not knowledge this idea I.E. That we are really an vital part of our environment, we fail to understand the effect which our sports have on it. Thus, the give up result is people feel unfastened to interrupt the surroundings for earnings, as they do not apprehend the impact they're having. Ultimately what takes region in nature, may even ultimately impact all of us human beings in exactly the same way.

They moreover believed that our inner nature connects people to others round them. When we broaden our ethical man or woman, we're dwelling according with the area spherical us, and in harmony with others. By evaluation, individuals who are not in contact with their very very very own real nature, are commonly in battle with others, and as a cease end result are alienated from the ones groups extra successfully.

Stoicism has stimulated rankings of prominent human beings eventually of facts, which includes kings and presidents. Thomas Jefferson come to be stated to have stored a reproduction of the works of Seneca on his bedside desk always. While George Washington reportedly located on a play about Cato, a Roman Senator who emerge as one of the maximum brilliant practitioners of Stoicism, in case you want to inspire his guys finally of the wintry weather they spent at Valley Forge.

If you are interested by working towards Stoicism, it is vital to bear in thoughts that it isn't always purported to be a technique to all of life's problems. Instead, it's far a tool which we're capable of use to become higher people. The famous adage which you shouldn't be wishing for an clean lifestyles, but as an alternative the electricity to undergo a hard one, couldn't be extra obvious proper right here. Stoicism in today's, is the proper intellectual automobile each person can use to make this a practicality of their ordinary lives.

## Chapter 2: Expectations and Demands – Dealing with Modern Day Life

"The essence of philosophy is that we should stay, just so our happiness depends as little as feasible on outside causes"

(Epictetus)

One of the proposed reasons to why Stoicism is gaining reputation another time, is to view its resurgence within the context of an increasingly more global. A world whose current conditions percentage many parallels with the big disarray which observed the demise of Alexander the Great. Many people are feeling unsure approximately the arena we stay in and the various problems we face, and are looking for more inexperienced coping mechanisms

Stoicism affords us with the device now not most effective to increase inner tranquility, however additionally to gather self-reliance, all even as analyzing how to act with distinctive feature in accordance with reason and commonplace experience.

For instance, it affords us a framework to address the numerous anxieties of current life, certainly through the usage of training us now not to fear about factors which may be past our manipulate. If this sounds acquainted to you, it's far because of the fact you have got were given probably heard of the Serenity prayer, which states "God, deliver me the serenity to simply accept what I can not change, the braveness to exchange the subjects I can, and the records to parent the distinction".

As Epictetus mentions inside the Enchiridion, "Some topics are up to us and a few aren't". He then asks what is to be completed, earlier than imparting the solution: "To make the tremendous of what is inside our manage, and to simply accept the rest because it takes area manifestly".

These education are ones which we ought to hold in mind even as we are faced with the severa troubles which we are going via nowadays. For example, we can be experiencing economic tension as to whether or now not or not we can be capable of find out a hobby, or to maintain at once to our present day-day one. Although it's miles our herbal inclination to fear, this is an unproductive feeling. Instead, we want to learn how to take a step again and observe the state of affairs in a more objective mild. This will allow us to decide what we CAN DO, and to weigh our options with grace and equanimity.

One ordinary scenario wherein a Stoic point of view is probably beneficial, is that of a motor twist of fate which became not our fault. Of path, our natural inclination is probably to get angry and begin shouting within the path of the alternative party. However you want to take a step decrease lower back and ask, "Would that help? Would it now not be better if I genuinely stepped out of the automobile, frivolously assessed the harm, and exchanged insurance records with the opposite riding strain?"

## The Art of Acquiescence

Stoicism also urges us not to absolutely take transport of our future, but as an opportunity gaining knowledge of to love what's taking place around us. As Epictetus places it, "Don't search for subjects to show up as you want they will, but instead choice that they arise as they really will – and then your lifestyles will flow properly". The time period for this kind of mind-set is the "Art of Acquiescence" and it essentially refers to developing the fine of a horrible state of affairs.

However it's also genuinely well really worth remembering that sometimes, what looks as if a setback, may also in the end, truely be a gain. For example, in 2008 LA Lakers train Phil Jackson needed to undergo surgical treatment to repair a hip damage which have been bothering him for a a number of years. During his healing length, he changed into restrained to a unique chair close to the gamers, and could now not walk across the court docket aspect as he end up so used to doing. Although Jackson became worried this could ward off his schooling, he decided that being on the sidelines above the participant's bench truely progressed his authority, and he have become able to assert himself with out being overbearing as he became in the beyond.

Avoiding the Materialism Trap

Another vital lesson we are able to examine, is to avoid putting an excessive amount of fee on fabric things. As Epictetus positioned it, "Wealth is composed not of having many possessions, however in having few wishes". Modern society has end up increasingly more materialistic, as smooth access to credit score rating gambling gambling playing cards and different varieties of customer credit score encourages us to spend increasingly more on luxuries and unique non-necessities, despite the truth that we don't have the cash to pay for them now.

After all, we will clearly pay for them later down the street, and we don't even need to pay the whole quantity. Advertising and mass media similarly encourage a way of life of materialism as we're constantly demonstrated lavish life which we're encouraged to aspire to. When we are provided with a today's colorful object (vehicle, residence, toy and lots of others) it creates a dissonance in our mind, to the factor of disappointment with the dearth of such possessions.

The most effective way to interrupt out from the materialism lure, is in reality to begin distinguishing amongst our desires and our dreams. We can without issues meet our desires, however our wishes may be countless. You want to break this "keeping up with the Jones" mentality to really unfastened your self from this awful highbrow spiral.

Marcus Aurelius, in his Meditations, states: "Do not take pleasure in desires of what you don't have, however rather depend wide variety amount the advantages you do own, after which preserve in thoughts with thanks how you could desire them inside the occasion that they have been now not yours". In extraordinary terms, we need to constantly domesticate an attitude of gratitude for what we've, in area of obsessing approximately what we do now not.

In our cutting-edge international we experience a full-size of dwelling which our grandparents, or maybe our parents might have observed no longer feasible. I'm no longer suggesting you want to rest on your laurels, or perhaps sense terrible about this reality. However maximum human beings must do properly to bear in mind this, and need to be appreciative of the benefits afforded to their contemporary state of affairs, which have been no longer to be had to others in the past.

Thus, we need to comply with Marcus Aurelius' recommendation and try and don't forget what existence might be like if we did no longer have the topics we take without any consideration now. For example, what if we were now not able to stay in a comfortable residence, or did not have a number of the creature comforts, collectively with a computer with Internet connection we're currently taking element in. Imagining now not having these items lets in us to understand them extra, so we aren't usually yearning for the things that we do now not have.

Learning How to Be Kind

Another cutting-edge hassle which the Stoics appeared to have anticipated is globalization. With advances in transportation and verbal exchange, the world seems smaller than it modified into inside the beyond. We can now speak with someone on the opposite element of the world in mins or perhaps seconds, and excursion to far-flung destinations in a bear in mind of hours. But current day traits in the direction of nationalism seems to be making international locations flip inward in desire to constructing ties with unique nations to create a truly global network.

According to Epictetus in his Discourses, at the identical time as you're asked the query of what u . S . A . You're from, do no longer say which you are from Athens or Corinth, however as an possibility that you are a "citizen of the arena". It is our alienation from each other, further to from nature, which has been the inspiration of most of the contemporary problems we're handling. These include climate exchange, huge income inequality and nearby displacement of societies due to global battle.

We can observe this mind-set on the micro stage as well, via seeking to be kinder to the human beings round us, even though they will be strangers or mere buddies. As Marcus Aurelius positioned it, "Injustice frequently lies no longer simply in what you're doing, but in what you are not doing". Inaction is regularly as awful as actively doing some thing risky. So if we are capable of perform acts of smooth kindness, even for people we don't understand, we are helping to sell justice within the global in our very own small manner.

## Chapter 3: Seneca – Dealing With Stressful Situations

"If you are distressed by using manner of some thing out of doors, the ache isn't always due to the issue itself, however for your estimate of it; and this you have got the strength to revoke at any moment"

(Marcus Aurelius)

During his lifetime, Seneca confronted a whole series of difficult conditions. In forty one BC, he became exiled to Corsica following accusations he had devoted adultery with the sister of the then-Emperor Caligula. He became allowed to go back eight years later to come to be the teach and advertising and marketing and marketing consultant to the Emperor Nero, who had nowadays ascended to the throne.

Unfortunately, Nero proved to be one of the most tyrannical emperors within the history of the Empire, and Seneca modified into forced to keep in his advisory feature, irrespective of requests from his camp to be allowed to retire.

Even after he retired from Nero's company, political intrigue persevered to hound Seneca. In 65 AD he have become accused of being worried inside the Pisonian Conspiracy, which have become a plot to assassinate Nero. Although he changed into truly innocent of the expenses, he was compelled and ordered to commit suicide.

Throughout those form of turbulent intervals of his life, however, Stoicism persisted to be a constant. However, he did no longer surely study and write at the philosophy, but also actively used it to help him navigate thru the numerous upsides and downsides of lifestyles. As a cease end result, he has become one of the most famous of the Stoic philosophers, with prominent figures together with entrepreneur Timothy Ferris and bestselling writer Nassim Taleb actively selling his works nowadays.

So what does Seneca have to say approximately coping with strain and locating happiness? The following is a sequence of reasons and his personal charges which better help us recognize his views in this.

"It is higher to laugh at lifestyles than to lament over it"

One of the principle reasons we enjoy confused is honestly because we take topics too appreciably. We want to learn how to test subjects of their right context. Many instances, what we see as an insurmountable trouble will appearance a good buy much less excessive after an exquisite night time time's sleep, or after letting a while pass.

We need to constantly consider that, whilst there are numerous conditions over which we have no control, we are capable of typically have manage over how we are capable of react to them. So we can choose to internalize subjects and make ourselves sense bad, or we are capable of choose to discover ways to snigger and release anxiety, enabling us to view them in a extra superb slight.

"Hardships enhance the mind as work does the frame"

Although we generally understand strain as being bad and counterproductive, in a few techniques it may be a exceptional emotion, counting on how we cope with it. As a Stoic, we should pick not to react with negative feelings to worrying situations and let them defeat us. Instead, we ought to discover ways to observe the scenario objectively, to peer how we are able to clear up it, and what we are able to take a look at from it.

Seneca himself illustrated the price of dealing definitely with stress within the course of his exile. Although he need to have felt intensely indignant thru the situation, he wrote a comforting letter to his mom, in preference to allowing himself to wallow in self-pity.

"The most effective is the person that has himself beneath control"

One of the tactics in which you can advantage happiness is to take manage of your very very own existence. Taking manipulate manner we should stay with self-control and no longer permit out of doors activities have an effect on us. This is illustrated with the aid of manner of the use of the tale of buddies, considered one of whom supplied a newspaper every day, and stated "real morning" to the information vendor. But the news provider never reacted, and eventually, the person's buddy requested, "Why do you preserve greeting him if he in no manner responds?" To which the individual then spoke back, "Why must I allow him impact how I behave?"

Thus, the lesson in this tale is that we need to do what is right with out being involved approximately what others are questioning, or how they'll be behaving. In truth, at the same time as we experience like we are in control, we enjoy the kind of inner self-generated happiness which cannot be matched with the resource of external validation from different human beings.

"There are extra topics to distress us than to harm us, and we go through greater in apprehension than truth"

One of the most remarkable resources of stress in peoples lives is the priority of things which MIGHT take region. We can all do not forget times whilst we also can have lain in mattress, no longer capable of sleep, and involved whether or not or now not we would even though have a venture, whether or no longer we are capable of have enough cash to make ends meet, and so on.

However, annoying approximately matters which we have no manipulate over will do us no ideal. It will high-quality bring about anxiety and vain internal struggling, which in flip could have an effect on our each day lives in a lousy way. Instead, we want to attention quality on the prevailing moment, rather than obsessing about what would probably appear in the destiny.

"A guy is fantastic as depressing as he thinks he's"

Much of the time, we take delivery of as actual with we is probably happy if best we were rich, handsome, had a better assignment and so forth. But the reality is, happiness is a preference we make. People who've the topics we aspire for, are regularly no happier than those who've a good buy an awful lot much less. On the alternative hand, there are various negative people who are glad because of the fact they may be contented with what they have, no matter how modest it is able to seem to us.

Thus, if we need to be glad, we want to select to be satisfied. This method gaining knowledge of to increase a extra excessive excellent thoughts-set toward existence. Of route, this is less difficult stated than executed, and it'll possibly take the time, however you may be happier ultimately with a super attitude instead of continuously living on the horrible topics which might occur.

"As long as you're alive, preserve gaining knowledge of a way to stay"

One of the most crucial misconceptions people have about existence, is that we stop gaining knowledge of the moment we end formal education. However the truth is, that is truely in which it starts. Life itself is the school this is normally in session, so pay interest. There is constantly a few aspect new we can research. All we need to do is alter the manner you check lifestyles to choose out up the ones lessons, to be open minded enough to take them in.

One of the great approaches someone can maintain reading from lifestyles, is to investigate out of your mistakes. Very frequently, we do some factor that we preference we hadn't achieved. Instead of truly feeling terrible approximately it, permit us to check the situation objectively and be conscious what we should have completed better, simply so we gained't make the identical mistake another time at the identical time as faced with a similar scenario.

"He who does actual to a few other person also does correct to himself"

Years in advance than Christ modified into born, Seneca and the Stoics were already education their very own version of the Golden Rule. Here, however, it is called the Law of Reciprocity, and it truely refers back to the notion that, you get once more what you supply. If you're type and generous to extraordinary humans, then you'll be rewarded in pass again, both without delay or in a roundabout manner.

However, you need to now not supply with the expectancy of having a few aspect in go returned, even though it's miles merely gratitude. After all, how precise humans react is beyond our control. Instead, we need to discover ways to provide for the sake of giving due to the fact it will in the long run bring us greater lasting inner happiness, which isn't dependent on the receiver's gratitude.

# Chapter 4: Problem Solving/Perseverance/Pragmatism Techniques

"He is most effective who has strength over himself"

(Seneca)

One severe example of approaches Stoicism can assist us endure even within the worst of situations, may be located within the inspiring story of James Stockdale. Stockdale modified into added to Epictetus through one in each of his professors while analyzing for his hold close's degree at Stanford, and it proved to be a lifestyles-converting occasion for him. From then on he always saved copies of the works of Epictetus on his bedside desk, regardless of in which he changed into assigned.

Stockdale served as a Naval pilot in a few unspecified time in the destiny of the Vietnam War, and whilst he changed into shot down in 1965 he became a prisoner of warfare. His first idea as he parachuted into the hands of his captors, changed into that he modified into entering the world of Epictetus. He turn out to be a captive for the following seven years and persisted everyday torture durations, but changed into able to muster up sufficient resistance that his captors needed to isolate him from the possibility prisoners.

During this ordeal, he drew energy from Stoic teachings together with "Work with what's internal your manipulate and your fingers will usually be whole". He served as a deliver of idea and control to the opportunity prisoners, such that they defied their captors thru refusing to confess to "crimes" they have been accused of or to bow to them in public. After he have grow to be launched from captivity, Stockdale became celebrated for this courage and manipulate even as he decrease returned domestic, and he have turn out to be one of the most famous advocates of Stoicism.

Of route, it is very probable that we're able to no longer stumble upon conditions this unstable or lifestyles threatening ourselves, but we are able to truly want to cope with many hard instances in our lives to a lesser amount. Stoicism can assist us to deal with them, even though it's miles certainly studying to view our situation in a more super way.

How to Develop Resilience

In his Letters from a Stoic, Seneca wrote to his buddy Lucilius Junior to propose an exercising to construct stability of mind and resilience. For 3 to four days at a time, he said, you need to stay as frugally as possible, eating most effective the most inexpensive food and carrying coarse clothing. Then, continuously ask your self, "Is this what I am frightened of?"

He encouraged doing this often, for as long as feasible, truly so it'd act as a check of person in area of being most effective a diversion from your every day life. Performing this exercising would feature a way to pork up your self without a doubt so on the identical time as you're confronted with a honestly tough state of affairs, you'll be able to deal with it lots more with out troubles.

Seneca likened this exercising to a soldier appearing maneuvers and making ready for struggle all through peacetime, so that after he genuinely needed to visit conflict, he may be capable of carry out his obligation with out difficulty. By turning into acquainted with what it technique to be terrible, you may apprehend that your peace of thoughts does not depend on fate on my own, when you recall that there may be typically enough to meet our needs.

Another mental exercise we're able to use to make bigger resilience is to expect losing some aspect or a person we view as relatively crucial to us. As Seneca factors out, "We can rob gift troubles of their strength via way of watching for their arrival in advance". You also can use this highbrow exercising to help you while you are going through a state of affairs along with beginning a ultra-modern business agency. By visualizing failure earlier, you may prevent yourself from becoming paralyzed through way of fear, as you realize that you may deal with the worst case situation from the outset.

As Marcus Aurelius located it in his Meditations, our purpose must be to come to be like the "headland, in which the waves continuously break, but which even though stands organisation even though the foaming waters churn spherical it." Instead of announcing, "It is my horrible fulfillment that this has passed off". Instead say "Although this has occurred to me, it's far my proper pinnacle fortune that I can go through it with out becoming distressed, neither being beaten thru the prevailing nor frightened of the future".

If all else fails, we're capable of remind ourselves of the way ephemeral matters certainly are. What looks like an insurmountable trouble in the moment will seem plenty less so after an remarkable night time time's sleep or a while has surpassed. In fact, we may additionally also be asking ourselves: What have been we so demanding approximately within the first place?

As Marcus Aurelius pointed out in his Meditations: "Look on the listing of all of those well-known those who felt excessive anger about a few component: the most famous, the most hated, a few aspect. Where are they now? Dust, smoke, fantasy – or not even a delusion. And keep in mind how trivial all the subjects we so passionately need are".

To help you develop this angle, you can try the highbrow workout called 'View From Above', the motive of this is to help you understand your characteristic in the massive network of humankind through the usage of letting you word the huge picture.

To do that workout, first discover a quiet location in which you may now not be disturbed. After interesting your body, start via becoming aware about your body as one organism or tool. Be detached and passive, and begin turning your hobby inward, as you turn out to be greater aware about your frame.

Now remember your self transferring upward and outward, and regularly broadening your attitude. First agree with which you see your self inside the context of the extra human interest spherical you. Then accept as true with which you see the city and then you definately simply see the Earth as you maintain moving upward.

As you do not forget your attitude broadening, ponder for your function in the greater context. You are without a doubt one maximum of the many billions of people on the planet. Then as you ponder the vastness of the universe, bear in mind how Earth is just absolutely one in all billions of planets, and like a speck of dust.

At the equal time, you need to view yourself as part of this bigger photograph. You are a crucial a part of the complete, your life is critical and the picks you're making are important. You understand that what you are making of your existence is the give up end result of your options. You allow trivial subjects fall away as you ponder what is in fact critical for your life.

Dealing With Difficult People

"When you awaken within the morning, tell yourself that I will encounter cranks, liars, busybodies, egomaniacs, ingrates and the jealous. These people are with their afflictions due to the truth they don't recognize the distinction among proper and evil."

This have become a part of how Marcus Aurelius organized to fulfill the day, via manner of reminding himself of all the silly characters he might in all likelihood meet. After all, he became emperor of Rome and his each day normal would possibly absolutely have consisted of conferences with a steady motion of these people.

Of path the above quote does no longer suggest he modified into judging them constantly. In reality, he proclaimed that with the aid of seeing each the ugliness of evil and the beauty of actual, the ones humans were despite the fact that "akin to me". But he talked about that "we're made for cooperation", and for this reason he might also must discover a manner to get along aspect them.

These phrases are some element that we ought to keep in mind in our every day encounters. We are positive to satisfy what we understand as "stupid" people, who do "silly" matters every time we get out of the residence. But we need to tell ourselves that we are not really so unique from them, besides for the choices we have have been given made. Thus, we want to domesticate staying strength and statistics whilst handling the ones tough people.

He furthermore pointed out that we should not determine humans for his or her man or woman flaws, however learn how to get hold of them for what they're. After all, we can not change them; they can simplest make the choice to alternate themselves. As Marcus mentioned, "You might possibly as well despise a fig tree for secreting juice".

Building Perseverance

In a letter to clearly one in each of his buddy Lucilius, Seneca referred to that a exceptional hassle which could most disturb us, is that of the unexpected. He stated that calamities are all the more extra while they arrive as a surprise.

Therefore, Seneca recommended we should put together ourselves with the useful resource of ensuring that no longer something is unexpected. We can do this via the use of looking ahead to the whole thing that may probably occur, in order that our minds may be fortified in competition to all contingencies. By mentally confronting those screw ups earlier than they stand up, they do not come as a wonder. So even as we are really faced via the use of them, we're able to realize that they will be no longer as terrible as we had predicted.

This highbrow exercising is surely the concept for the Cognitive Behavioral approach referred to as "decatastrophizing". This method is meant to address tension as a consequence of perceived future sports, basically while blowing topics out of percentage. For example, an worker can also worry that inside the event that they've been to make a small mistake at artwork, it's going to bring about them being allow move.

Thus, the manner to challenge these irrational mind is largely to play a pastime of 'what if?' What if I did lose my interest? What if I did make the mistake? What's the greater excessive that would seem? What may want to I do subsequent? The purpose of asking and answering those questions is that will help you address the final results and guarantee you that, in spite of the truth that the worst does seem, it isn't always the stop of the area. Thus, you could recognise that you can stay on or perhaps achieve achievement over the worst case scenario.

Another approach for developing perseverance and inner power is to use the 'reserve clause' highbrow exercise. When you create a reserve clause you're basically admitting that, irrespective of how tough you figure, the final consequences is essentially past your control. For instance, at the equal time as we're making ready for a assignment interview, we are able to do all the education that we are able to, however nevertheless now not get the manner.

Why is this? There are really factors that we're able to by no means expect and for that reason, can not prepare for in advance. For example, the character doing the hiring may have determined that the opportunity candidate became a higher in form for the place than we had been.

Thus, while you've completed together along with your coaching, and you experience assured for your potential to prevail, you really want to surrender to the scenario. The purpose of this is not to allow you to off the hook in case topics do not skip nicely, but as a substitute to simply accept that there are elements which is probably beyond your control. Thus, you could prepare your self mentally for the very last outcomes, or create a Plan B, in an strive to inform you what to do subsequent.

As Seneca puts it, "The smart guy is concerned simplest with the motive of his actions, no longer their results; beginnings are internal our energy, however the very last outcomes is in the end as plenty as Fortune".

## Chapter 5: Daily Stoic Meditations and Affirmations

"Never allow the destiny disturb you. You will meet it, when you have to, with the equal weapons of cause which these days arm you towards the present"

(Marcus Aurelius)

If you want to begin residing like a Stoic, the notable way to acquire this is to enlarge a every day ordinary of meditations and affirmations. By meditating each day on costs from the classical Stoic masters, you could start internalizing them a good way to follow them to the tough existence situations you face on a every day foundation.

You can start your day with a Morning Meditation, which you need to carry out because the first actual detail you do, as speedy as you rise. Start with the aid of taking a couple of minutes to put together and compose yourself, then keep to do one of the following:

Meditate on a specific Stoic principle. One of the maximum well-known tenets is truely to remind your self to just accept that there are topics you'll face which might be beyond your manage. Thus, you have to decide to focus at the subjects that you could manage, which embody identifying to behave as a fantastic character regardless of what takes vicinity.

Prepare for the day beforehand with the useful resource of way of going to a quiet vicinity and then meditating for a couple of minutes. If you're exterior, you can quietly stare upon the growing sun or you may close to your eyes and attention your awesome senses on what goes on round you. If you may't or don't need to transport out of doors, you can in reality sit down on the point of your mattress or on the floor in a snug function.

Quietly slip proper right into a mindfulness meditation to help calm your thoughts and clean it from any distractions or needless chatter. All you want to do is consciousness on the present 2d for longer and longer durations of time, focusing to your senses and your respiratory to assist middle you.

Choose a selected Stoic one of a kind feature, which encompass justice, moderation or braveness, that you would like to cultivate. Then consider a sure situation which you may encounter for your every day regular, then don't forget how you can workout this unique function within the face of it.

In addition to morning meditations, you should moreover be doing all your Evening Meditations. This exercise is supposed as a manner to assess how you have were given had been given practiced Stoicism during the day, in that you fell short and in what areas you want development. As Epictetus placed it in his Discourses, quoting Pythagoras:

"Do not allow yourself to go to sleep until you have were given reckoned all of the deeds you have got accomplished at some level inside the daytime. Ask your self: Where did I fall short? What did I do? What have I left undone? Then scold yourself for cowardly acts and feature a laugh in those acts you've got completed nicely".

Before going to sleep, take five to 10 minutes to check the activities of the day. You can use the subsequent as manual questions:

• Did you permit your movements at some diploma inside the day to be dominated via irrational fears or by immoderate dreams?

• How had been you able to have a examine Stoic thoughts or virtues? What development did you're making in living a Stoic existence?

• Where did you fall short in living up to Stoic standards? In what regions might also want to you've got had been given completed better? Did you leave out any possibilities to workout Stoic virtues?

You should moreover maintain in mind keeping a Philosophical Journal. Keeping a magazine is an effective method for ingraining the concepts of Stoicism so that you can call on them at the same time as needed.

The motive of the mag is to will let you look at what has happened for your lifestyles, so you can turn out to be aware of shortcomings and to music how your perspective adjustments over time. You can use the Meditations of Marcus Aurelius as your version for a manner to create your journal.

One of the most critical things you can do in this magazine is the Examination of Conscience. This Examination includes not looking for acts which have made you feel responsible, due to the reality they violate a few shape of spiritual code, however as an alternative seeking out times within the path of the day in which you fell quick of dwelling as lots as Stoic principles.

The Philosophical Journal will because of this encompass commands you have decided at the equal time as doing an Examination. First do the Examination mentally, and then write down some thing education you take from it.

Although you may do that exercising on the end of the day, it isn't always recommended which you obtain this, at the same time as you endure in thoughts which you could probably neglect what has passed off. Instead, carry out the Examination on a second-to-2d basis as critical, after which write down what you need to as it arises.

After you've got were given completed this, you need to forgive yourself thru the usage of letting cross of the person you've got been at the same time as this stuff passed off, consequently do no longer be too difficult on your self. Remember this character truely completed those deeds due to a lower level of interest. Since this particular individual is now vain, you will be free to stay as this new person in the morning.

Stoic Meditations

"No man or woman definitely offers their cash to passersby, but too without difficulty do we surrender our lives. We're miserly with coins and belongings, and however we assume now not something of losing time, the one detail we need to all be tight-fisted over."

In this passage from Seneca's On the Brevity of Life, we're reminded that we should value our time. Ironically, however, we are living in an age wherein there are extra distractions than ever, and greater techniques for humans to get in touch with us, even when we are out of the residence. Virtually anybody has a cell smartphone or a pill, and we are anticipated to typically be available, and to answer calls and messages right away.

Unfortunately, this has resulted inside the erosion of what became our personal time.

When we had been given domestic, it changed into anticipated that we might completely offer our interest to our families and our cherished ones. But nowadays, bosses and friends feel they're able to freely penetrate what need to be our personal space.

Thus, we want to be greater vigilant in protecting our personal time and our non-public obstacles. While we will earn extra money, we can't earn greater time, so we should try to waste as little of it as humanly possible.

"This is the sign which you have perfected your man or woman – that you spend every day as if it have been your remaining, without pretending, laziness or frenzy."

In this quote from Marcus Aurelius' Meditations, he reminded us of perhaps the maximum crucial precept of Stoicism – to continuously stay in the present. The task which continually faces us is a way to incredible spend our time and our lives. But there may be an inclination inside us to generally positioned aside thoughts approximately our mortality, and to tell ourselves that there can be generally the next day. But what if there had been no tomorrow?

Thus, the venture a Stoics need to face is, a way to stay our exceptional lives, every single day. If we died at sundown, can also we've were given the functionality to mention to ourselves: I lived my super life nowadays? This is what we ought to constantly attempt for.

"It is not that there's too short a time to stay, however that we squander loads of our lives. We are given lifestyles in enough diploma that we can do many stuff if we spend it properly. But at the equal time as existence is poured down the drain of forget and luxury, when we lease it to no correct cause, then we ultimately understand that it has exceeded us with the useful resource of the use of with out even noticing it passing. We don't get a quick life – we make it quick."

Another passage from On the Brevity of Life reminds us of the significance of spending our lives appropriately. How commonly have we said to ourselves that life is just too short? Seneca reminds us that it isn't the time that you have that is important, but the way you spend it. Think of what number of humans we have got heard of who have completed a lot at a young age. While we're able to't all be like that, we are able to decide what we actually need to do with our lives and spend our time strolling on it, in place of wasting our lives doing unnecessary subjects.

"People look for retreats in the hills, with the aid of the coast or within the u.S.A., and you too are specially predisposed to experience this. But this isn't philosophical, thinking about the truth that you could retreat into yourself at any time you want. There isn't always any region that someone can discover a extra problem-loose and peaceful retreat than within his own thoughts."

This quote from Marcus Aurelius' Meditations reminds us that we don't need to exit of town, or perhaps leave the residence, to revel in a personal retreat. One of the most vital Stoic highbrow wearing sports is that of the self-retreat, which you can use as a method for self-discovery. All you want is to devote 5 to 10 minutes a day to wandering round internal your private mind. You can visualize being in a favorite place, which include the seaside or the mountains, in which you experience at peace and you could calm your thoughts.

"When you are finding it hard to awaken early inside the morning, suppose this: 'I am getting as a whole lot as do a person's artwork. Do I regardless of the reality that resent getting up if I am going out to do that which I even have come to be born for and brought into this worldwide? Or have emerge as I framed for this, to hold myself warmth with the aid of the use of the usage of mendacity beneath the bedclothes?"

This passage from Marcus Aurelius' Meditations reminds us that it's miles vital for us to do our obligation and fulfill our duties. Apart from our non-public and expert obligations, we also have a more responsibility to others, in order to collect a better society and to make the world a better region. This is why one of the vital Stoic disciplines is Philanthropy, whose extraordinary feature is Action.

Although most human beings be given as real with philanthropy first-rate includes giving to charity, to a Stoic it also refers to taking motion for the common gain of all. This can involve taking part in community efforts or running with advocacy companies to make certain a more simply society. For a Stoic, philanthropy involves being lively, rather than passive, if you want to help bring about first-class alternate. But we ought to not decide others who fall short of this quality, because of the fact that we're all flawed in any case.

## Chapter 6 : Other Day-to-Day Stoic Tips of a Spy

"Progress is not performed via suitable fortune or accident, but through strolling on yourself every day"

(Epictetus)

Having checked out a number of the conventional mind of Stoicism, and the commonplace techniques human beings use to place them into region. I desired to encompass a financial ruin to highlight some of my non-public critiques while living out this existence philosophy. It is not any mystery that participants of the CIA are placed via rigorous training to construct every bodily and highbrow durability.

Looking decrease lower back on it, I can see my time present process this training, similarly to the time spent in worrying conditions in the difficulty, were all individual constructing tales which certainly molded me proper into a actual Stoic. The following are a number of the maximum pertinent factors I accept as true with it vital to recognition on and expand if you are attempting to do the same:

Immediate Attention

The first and primary trick is to deal with paintings which calls for immediate interest. This will take a few making plans to pick out exactly what the ones duties are, but it will be a well without a doubt properly worth the effort. Say as an instance you end that particular emails and correspondence want to be spoke back to right away. Do so without losing in addition time.

It is a mistake to push the ones responsibilities to a later factor as this can lessen their price, and greater importantly result in a sense of laziness toward them. It's realistic to get into the habit of finishing those vital moves as quick as they arrive up, because of the fact the massive majority of development you will make over the longer term will come from those duties.

Tough first

Along the equal strains to the above principle, you may discover that the topics on the manner to make the maximum crucial distinction to your lifestyles will often be the toughest, and the topics you can least need to do. This wont constantly be the case I.E. The hardest challenge will garner the finest payoff, however this 80/20 fashion questioning (wherein 20% of your paintings will create type of 80% of your effects) is a first rate region to base your thinking.

So after you've got completed the proper away movement obligations, it's time to move onto the extra everyday sports activities. Here it's far going to be crucial to address the hard ones first earlier than moving onto the a lot less complicated obligations. This will appear a chunk daunting at the begin however as you get aware of prioritizing the most tough and critical sports first, it'll speedy grow to be 2nd nature to you.

As constantly hold in thoughts to make a listing of the numerous sports activities to have a observe in an afternoon after which set up them primarily based mostly on their diploma of issue. Tackle the tough or complicated sports activities first, if you have the maximum physical and mental energy to perform that, making sure which you are left with enough time to finish up the simpler ones that can be wiped easy up with a lot much less attempt.

Urgency

Create a sense of urgency with each challenge which you absorb so you have the risk to finish it clearly and on time. As I described above, make a list and grade your responsibilities so as of importance and trouble and deal with the sports on the top of the listing first.

A super trick is to reduce the time limit on every occasion so you are capable to finish the interest in the fastest time feasible without rushing it. Schedule a time for every of the sports activities after which pursue them for that reason.

Rise early

One of the maximum essential suggestions to comply with so that it will manifestly extend a Stoic attitude is getting up early within the morning. It can be noticeably critical so as to upward thrust up by way of the usage of five-6am as a way to have sufficient time to workout, plan your day, and make your self a healthful breakfast.

Those who rise later within the day are positive to be more harassed, and give up their day on a awful look at. Simply waking an hour earlier than regular and planning the day ride can with out issue keep away from this tendency. In order to rise up earlier, you may moreover should sleep in advance and so it's miles going to be quality to hit the bed at the least an hour earlier than you'll generally do. Skip indulging in distractions earlier than drowsing as they might disturb this pattern extensively.

Find Inspiration

It is notably crucial to be inspired to carry out a assignment a superb way to beautify productivity. Stoicism is essentially a shape of Self-Discipline, that may be a phrase that conjures up a revel in of motivation, tough paintings and in the long run unrelenting self-control to gain. However, it is a fantasy that power of mind desires such immoderate tiers of try and accumulate.

Motivation is fleeting and will ultimately fail you. If there can be one thing which I honestly have located over the years (in lots of compromising situations) is which you require concept for the critical stuff you need to benefit or trade about your lifestyles.

True self-discipline emerges at the same time as an intrinsic "why" involves the fore, thereby pushing a person within the route of pursuing their internal most desires. If someone looks like what they need to obtain is inspiring or critical sufficient, then they will robotically make bigger a self-disciplined and Stoic mind-set in the direction of achieving it. It truely turns into the path of least resistance.

People who can do that almost constantly discover that it turns into much less complex to pursue their targets and chase their desires. Try to spend 1/2-hour a day reflecting upon these dreams which ought to help you domesticate this concept for reaching them.

Don't multitask

Multitasking is in no manner a extremely good concept because it reduces your interest on the venture on hand, which in the long run reduces productiveness for the most factor. Pay hobby and consciousness in on truly one issue at a time and keep away from the temptation to tackle too many stuff proper now. People presume they're being extra efficient, that could be a fantasy. Most humans are simply busy...

If there are various sports to undertake then stack them one after any other and flow about them in an orderly fashion ticking off every in advance than trying the following. I find out this allows domesticate a thoughts-set for completing responsibilities properly, giving them the ok time a hobby they require. I promise you, doing matters nicely from the outset, will prevent masses extra time in the end.

## Chapter 7: The Tragedy That Gave Birth to Stoicism

Stoicism's beginnings passed off in a grieving Athens. The dying of Aristotle and Alexander the Great, which took place on consecutive years, created a void in the common philosophy of the town-nation. With the demise of these icons, got here the gradual but positive descent of aspirations and philosophies aiming for the success of a utopic society and a grand or great existence. As a quit result, Athens now not modified into at the center of the area's interest. Its very own brand of cultural prominence and urbanity, which made it the focal point of global attraction, has spread and made its manner to cities together with Alexandria, Pergamum, and Alexandria.

Along with this, the formerly installation community rule have grow to be modified with governors who have been faraway and have been sponsored by way of the usage of way of large political segments. The barrier that separated the barbarian and the Greek modified into toppled as tribal and provincial gadgets were torn aside, which Alexander had started out out and emerge as determined by way of manner of the Romans. The deterioration of the concept of a unfastened man and the eventual upward push of blind loyalty and morally missing obedience to a ruler, emerge as hastened via topics and normal humans dropping their personal freedom. This occasion recommended company and rendering of timeless loyalty to a pacesetter whose morality held no ground in his characteristic.

Order had now been changed with the useful resource of political and social chaos, as conventional virtues were overtaken via unsure and ephemeral values. Stoicism rose inside the changing worldwide, masses to like how our world is now, wherein former codes of morality and theories of expertise have become feebler at the same time as being applied to the problems that plague our international in recent times.

Stoicism is derived from the Stoa Poikile in which its founder, Zeno of Citium, decided on to maintain his public lectures. As you have got take a look at with the aid of now, Zeno's discovery and founding of Stoicism became introduced about through the use of an unlucky and especially tragic come upon with future. He lost all of his possessions and fortune in a shipwreck whilst crusing. After which, he decided to spend his time in a ebook area in choice to moping. In this window-shopping for-to-keep away from-moping-interest of types, Zeno picked up some of Socrates' books.

There and there, he commenced out to digest each argument, symposium, and declarations written in Socrates' books. After being intrigued with the resource of the ensures and the philosophies he had simply observe, he right now sought to satisfy the town's maximum referred to philosophers to investigate similarly near the way in which it become top notch to stay his lifestyles. In this frantic are seeking for, Zeno stumbled into Crates of Thebes. Crates have emerge as his first mentor in his quest to apprehend and in the end growth his very very very own philosophies.

After being a scholar of Crates, Stilpo, Philo, Xenocrates, Polemo, and Diodorus Cronus, Zeno set his eyes on being a teacher as well. Zeno began out his public lectures speakme on the colonnade inside the Agora of Athens, which is also known as the Stoa Poikile. Initially, his disciples named themselves the Zenonians, but later diagnosed themselves as Stoics, which become without a doubt a call formerly attributed to poets who convened at the Stoa Poikile.

Stoicism from the very starting became all approximately personal ethics guided by means of a machine of good judgment with a recognize within the course of the herbal global and the rationality of its abilities. To similarly apprehend this philosophy, one need to be aware of the phrase Eudaimonia, due to this blessedness or happiness. According to Stoicism, the direction towards Eudaimonia as social beings is guided via way of the recognition of and not permitting oneself to be the difficulty of various emotions which incorporates worry of ache or preference for satisfaction.

Along with this, the course to Eudaimonia entails a rational records of the arena by way of using manner of doing one's element in adhering to nature's plan, which includes running with and treating others with justice and equity. To located it into easy phrases, Stoicism goals us to be higher human beings. Rather than desiring to be a catalyst or a motion icon, this philosophy goals us to take a step lower back and begin by using way of improving ourselves first, earlier than aspiring for worldwide alternate.

The Stoics emphasised the education of fantastic function as the exceptional correct for humans, and that some component out of doors of it—which consist of satisfaction, wealth or health—are neither horrible nor accurate on their private. What they endorse with the resource of that is that particular characteristic is the high-quality element taken into consideration to be in easy terms suitable, and that each one the alternative topics in our life—cash, smartphones, or a six-%—are not genuinely terrible or exquisite of their very personal rights however as an opportunity may be substances for which right or terrible topics can upward thrust up from. As a depend variety of reality, this philosophy or tool of morality, at the aspect of Aristotelian ethics, has fashioned one of the founding and crucial techniques to Western unique characteristic ethics.

With this, the Stoics moreover emphasised that risky feelings got here from judgement mistakes. Having stated so, the Stoics believed that one should aspire to maintain will, or as they referred to as it: prohairesis, it absolutely is according with nature. Thus, for the Stoics, an example of someone's philosophy and belief modified into no longer heard thru the terms they'll be pronouncing however as an opportunity may be visible in how they behaved. Which, if idea of a 2d time, the Stoic deduces that if every person's conduct isn't always in step with their philosophies, they're additionally then no longer regular with nature. For them, will is the wall that maintained the standards of 1's virtues and that which stored someone's philosophies, morality, and notion in line with nature. If this wall is breached, then comes the errors in judgement which ultimately result in the detrimental emotions that not nice purpose harm to others but most significantly, to oneself.

## The Three Great Stoic Sages

Stoics which includes Seneca, Epictetus, and Marcus Aurelius emphasized that distinctive feature on my own may be sufficient for Eudaimonia, which then allowed a Stoic to be emotionally proof towards any of the unfavourable feelings introduced up with the aid of manner of misfortune and misery. It is high-quality at some point of this difficulty wherein a sage, a term this is used to become aware of a Stoic, can fine be deemed to be in reality and in the end loose from vicious ethical corruptions.

Having already said Seneca, Epictetus, and Marcus Aurelius, it is excellent turning into that their lives be showcased in order to further see the existence in the returned of a sage.

Lucius Annaeus Seneca the Younger

The life of Lucius Annaeus Seneca the Younger (as his father additionally had the identical name) commenced out in Corbuda, Spain. He then moved to Rome in which he become knowledgeable every in philosophy and rhetoric. His father changed proper right into a former Roman knight who later grew to grow to be writer and trainer of rhetoric. His mom, Helvia, changed into a diagnosed member of the Baetician family. His first come upon with Stoicism got here within the shape of the School of Sextii and its humans Attalus, Sotion and Papirius Fabianus. After being delivered to Egypt collectively with his aunt and eventually returning to Rome, Seneca became able to strong a seat within the Roman Senate thank you in element and keen on his aunt's have an impact on as being a shape of bridge among Egypt and Rome.

Seneca's existence as a Stoic can be taken into consideration as a paradox. The man changed into considered to be one of the wealthiest human beings in the Roman Empire as he modified into additionally a excessive-score economic clerk on the element of being a senator. However, his lifestyles grew to grow to be for the worst at the same time as he modified into exiled to Corsica by using way of way of Emperor Claudius after being accused of adultery. After his exile, the mother of future Emperor and tyrant Nero, Aggripina, asked for Seneca's return to turn out to be Nero's private display and adviser.

Much of Seneca's fortune came from being an adviser to Nero. Ironically, his death moreover came in the fingers of Nero, who asked him to devote suicide. Throughout all of this, Stoicism remained as a steady associate for Seneca. For Seneca, to live a Stoic existence meant that lets in you to think a way through the awful conditions in existence thru searching at the extreme aspect and reading to go through such hardships through dwelling with a tremendous.

Seneca noticed this contemporary day inside the form of an Anchor. He encouraged his buddy Lucillus, to select a function model as an anchor for the standards of methods life need to be lived. Seneca furthermore became a man who modified into no longer a slave of his wealth. Although being a super instance of a paradox of possessions and philosophy, Seneca changed into someone who in no manner tied himself tightly to his riches. He modified into keen in taking component within the upside delivered approximately thru having riches, however made powerful that it changed into to be used on every occasion critical, and in no way genuinely rely upon it for happiness. Seneca famously wrote in On The Happy Life:

"For the clever man does now not don't forget himself unworthy of any provides from Fortune's fingers: he does no longer love wealth but he may instead have it; he does not admit into his coronary coronary heart however into his home; and what wealth is his he does no longer reject but continues, wishing it to deliver more scope for him to workout his one in all a type feature."

Epictetus

Epictetus' lifestyles is also one that begs hobby. Compared to Marcus Aurelius and Seneca, this guy changed into the wonderful proof of residing a lifestyles as a Stoic. Epictetus have become a slave. Epictetus end up born in Hierapolis, which is understood in recent times to be Turkey, as a slave beneath Epaphroditus' own family. Epaphroditus allowed Epictetus to have a look at liberal research amidst being a slave. Through this, he modified into capable of find out the Stoic Philosophy.

Musonius Rufus, a sage as well, taught him and have become his mentor inside the course of his childhood. After obtaining his freedom, he started training in Rome. After 25 years, destiny did no longer smile upon Epictetus as he modified into banished with the aid of Emperor Domitian collectively with all philosophers in Rome. Epictetus became pressured to escape to Nicopolis in Greece wherein he lived out the relaxation of his days training at a philosophy college he had primarily based.

Epictetus opens up his ebook, The Enchiridion, with one of the most crucial proverbs ever in Stoic philosophy. He stated:

"Some matters are in our control and others not. Things in our manipulate are opinion, pursuit, desire, aversion, and, in a word, anything are our non-public movements. Things no longer in our manipulate are frame, belongings, reputation, command, and, in a unmarried word, some thing aren't our very very own moves."

This serves as a reminder to never be disillusioned or angered via the matters we haven't any manage over which incorporates outdoor incidents, and one-of-a-kind humans's evaluations. In a way, this precise reminder permits us takes topics in simply, by means of way of remembering that regardless of what happens, we need to constantly take consolation in knowing that we are able to generally allow go of the matters we can not manage.

Another teaching which Epictetus is quite famous for is his belief in prescribing oneself a person to attain a aim or an high-quality character. He notes that the idea of prescribing oneself a person allows maintain ourselves in take a look at during instances whilst we act instinctively out of addiction. He argues that regardless of the fact that it may be tough, it allows in reminding us and maintaining us business enterprise as we artwork towards our desires in life.

Marcus Aurelius

Lastly but glaringly now not the least is Marcus Aurelius. Marcus Aurelius have become born a no person notwithstanding being a member of a wonderful and hooked up family in Rome. His call satisfactory gained traction while he have become accompanied thru way of Antoninus, a senator inside the direction of Hadrian's time as emperor and who changed into slated to become an emperor. After the lack of lifestyles of Hadrian and the eventual rule and dying of Antoninus, it become Marcus' time to take the diploma. He co-ruled with Lucius Verus, his followed brother, for over decades till his demise. Marcus' reign changed into full of stressful conditions which includes the wars with the barbarian tribes and the Parthian Empire, at the facet of the upward push of Christianity and the plague devastated Rome.

Stoicism, for Marcus Aurelius, supplied him with a framework as to how he have to deal with the every day demanding conditions that got here his manner because the chief of one of the global's maximum feared and advanced civilizations. Marcus embraced Stoicism after he observed out of it from his mentors and instructors. He modified into eager on his mentor Rusticus, who additionally had introduced him to Epictetus. Perhaps the maximum vital tragedy of Marcus Aurelius got here after his loss of life, on the identical time as his philosophies and teachings were thrown to the side by using the usage of using the usa and empire he took care of till his very last breath. Luckily for him, the whole worldwide is there to pick out out up in which he left off.

Marcus Aurelius' Meditations serves as on the terrific portions of literature ever made, and possibly the first-rate of its type. It gave us a peek into the intimate and private mind of the world's as quick as only guy. Among such mind is his introspection and his steady advising in the course of himself at the way to follow up on his responsibilities and supply properly for his obligations. Of the numerous instructions Marcus Aurelius has handed down in this e-book, there are in which we are able to right now look at from and exercise to our lives.

First is his notion of practicality in relation to our virtues. Marcus Aurelius believed that we is probably greater efficient if we spend most of our time practicing the virtues we've got got or maybe the topics we are correct at, in area of moping round and wallowing in self-pity about the things we cannot do. He said:

"No one must ever accuse you of being brief-witted.

All right, however there are plenty of various topics you may't claim you 'haven't had been given in you.' Practice the virtues you can show: honesty, gravity, staying power, austerity, resignation, abstinence, patience, sincerity, moderation, seriousness, high-mindedness. Don't you see how hundreds you need to offer—beyond excuses like 'can't'? And but you still accept lots less."

Another key takeaway from the lifestyles of the previous Roman Emperor is that we want to learn how to depend upon others. As were referred to in advance, this guy co-dominated his empire beside his adopted brother. As a cease cease result, they had been able to offer Rome with arguably considered one in each of its superb eras. In Meditations he stated that:

"When you need encouragement, consider the talents the human beings round you've got: this one's energy, that one's modesty, another's generosity, and so on. Nothing is as encouraging as whilst virtues are visibly embodied in the human beings spherical us, on the identical time as we're almost showered with them. It's nicely to hold this in thoughts."

Having have a look at the lives of Zeno and the 3 high-quality sages of Stoicism, it is secure to say that during case you are despite the fact that doubting your self at this issue if Stoicism is definitely for you, then you definately sincerely are quite unsuitable. If Stoicism changed into capable of do what it did for Zeno (a person who in fact lost the entirety), Seneca (whose lifestyles has lengthy lengthy gone through such a number of united states of america of america of americaand downs, and in reality have become a mentor to a tyrant), Epictetus (the man born as a slave), and Marcus Aurelius (who have turn out to be considered to be one of the handiest men ever), then this e-book can also do the same for you.

## Chapter 8: Virtues of Stoicism

Wisdom and Temperance served the Stoics properly. Marcus Aurelius is the pinnacle instance of such. In the film Gladiator, we see a glimpse of such tendencies in an elder emperor version of Aurelius. But this model, which is probably the cause of why many humans in recent times are familiar collectively alongside together with his call, is but a tiny grain of salt within the whole pool of excellence in each Temperance and Wisdom Marcus Aurelius possesses.

If one meditates, pun meant, truly on what his lifestyles has been and what he has been capable of advantage, then I suppose at least one would come to apprehend the gravity of strain the character had confronted. Marcus Aurelius have become so influential for his display of discipline for every Temperance and Wisdom, that YouTube motion photos are being made to actually recommendation human beings on the way to wake up like Marcus Aurelius, a way to sleep like Marcus Aurelius, a manner to eat like Marcus Aurelius, how to lead like Marcus Aurelius, and so forth.

This goes to expose that a number of people look as a whole lot as this guy given the notice he possessed. One have to no longer pick an anecdote approximately Marcus Aurelius and make that suitable for him at the manner to recognize Aurelius because the Stoic. If one without a doubt wants to dedicate time into now not first-class expertise however furthermore statistics the character within the back of certainly one of Rome's excellent eras, it is superb that they examine everything of his ebook: The Meditations.

You see, it became Marcus Aurelius himself who said that during case you pick out to be accurate at some factor, then bypass forth and difficulty yourself in doing so. In the equal way, the same suitable judgment ought to be done in reading about Stoicism and the humans inside the again of it. Don't assume that once analyzing this ebook, you can come out as a complete-blown Stoic yourself. The reality is, possibly you may no longer. But that's exact sufficient.

It is the sacrifice for selecting control. Control, if you ask any Stoic, is constrained. There is only a few matters you may manipulate throughout his/her existence. Such is lifestyles. The suitable information even though is that the Ancient Stoics have supplied us with 4 virtues which we need to attempt to control and grasp, with a purpose to maximize the bounds of what we are able to manipulate. The first some of the four, are expertise and temperance. Perhaps, those are the most important out of all the virtues, thinking about that they go with the flow hand in hand in guiding the following two.

Epictetus as soon as stated:

"The leader assignment in lifestyles is certainly this: to find out and separate topics so that I can say sincerely to myself which can be externals not below my manage, and which want to do with the options I clearly manage. Where then do I look for correct and evil? Not to uncontrollable externals, however interior myself to the alternatives which are my personal"

Philosophy's that means is the love of knowledge. For the Stoics, no longer simplest do they have got a love for records but furthermore an innate desire to pursue and exercising it inside the path of their lives on a each day basis. The Stoics believed that information is the understanding of what to pick out, what no longer to live a ways from, and what's neither. Thus, a Stoic's movements are absolutely knowledgeable with the resource of this information.

The motive in which know-how is one of the maximum critical exceptional function of they all, together with temperance, is as it informs not best movement but is likewise knowledgeable with the aid of the understanding, the studying, and the enjoy one has in this worldwide. As it have been in historical times, human beings nowadays should look at to differentiate what can be useful in dwelling an great lifestyles, and what cannot be. That is basically the workout of statistics for a Stoic.

Epictetus additionally has stated which you cannot examine that which you count on you realize. Which is going to expose that aside from figuring out to recognize and analyze, a stoic need to be capable of apprehend if he/she has the right experience to lower back up an current know-how or to warrant a much more wanted studying close to some component she or he claims statistics of. As you may probably see with the aid of now, information isn't always essentially a complicated first-rate feature. It is fairly simple, to be honest. This does no longer advocate that it is straightforward. Stoicism dares to say that know-how, even though being the vital and theoretical backbone of the philosophy, cannot be really decided out if it is not used with courage, temperance, and justice.

As it's far with all the four virtues, nobody survives by myself and creates a percentage of what you could anticipate to be, as a Stoic. Learning or training one isn't always enough. In the case of knowledge, we need in case you want to discover ways to observe it for the relaxation of the virtues. For example, we want to be courageous in all of our pursuits. Wisdom, on this experience, serves as compass for our braveness. It allows us to pinpoint the critical subjects or goals we want to learn or collect in our lives.

For justice, knowledge serves because the eyes that see thru what is at the surface. The cause within the again of that is because of the reality justice in itself, warrants equity. And if we are to deal with everybody with justice and kindness, then we have to understand the cause in the back of. Wisdom determines what we need to aim to look in each exclusive and what we need to placed to the component and push aside as it is unnecessary and negative to our imaginative and prescient of justice.

Lastly, for temperance. Wisdom is like temperance's prolonged-misplaced brother, and manipulate's cousin. The reason in which the three standards are framed is due to the truth it's miles not feasible for one to exist without the other, similar to the four virtues. Wisdom makes temperance paintings in giving it the blueprint as to what need to be exercised with manipulate and as a great deal as what aspect need to or no longer it's. Given this information, we now see know-how certainly. The cause why it's far essential is due to the fact the rest of the virtues won't art work with out it.

Practical Application

For you to exercise records and ensure that it enables you in your every day lifestyles, Stoicism shows which you start with the small topics. Embrace the small matters which you already apprehend that you control. An instance is your ingesting behavior. Although it'd sound as a cliché, but technically it's miles actual. You can control your eating conduct. And hence, you're informed of what you're or what you aren't consuming.

Therefore, to workout understanding in this case, you want to first determine your motive. Do you need a healthy body? Do you need to be muscular? Do you want to be buff? Do you need to be toned? Or do you want to be a sumo wrestler? You determine this with know-how, given the know-how of a aim's necessity or no longer. After that you then determine what sort of healthy dietweight-reduction plan or exercising plan you can positioned into impact for the stated reason.

At this factor, it's miles all quite easy for you because of the fact there may be a ton of statistics at the net regarding this. What is crucial here with reference to expertise is on the same time as you're absolutely sitting within the sofa, finished with exercise and accomplished in conjunction with your prescribed eating regimen meal for dinner. This is in which true knowledge comes in. You want to look at and know what it is that you could manage or now not. You have to study your enjoy with the idea of manipulate. Then you look decrease returned at yourself. You now decide whether or not you'll skip for that ice cream cake your pal left for you within the fridge or no longer, and surely rest easy for each other day of workout tomorrow.

You see, records has never been approximately making the right desire. It is ready what is making the proper desire for your self. It is set understanding yourself, reading yourself, and being attentive to your evaluations. Whatever you may choose to do whether or now not or not to eat or to sleep in the instance given above, you need to be on top of factors and moreover you need to be at peace with the selection you surely made. As peace, particularly with oneself, is the tremendous proof of statistics in someone.

Temperance

Now we keep to Temperance. Temperance is pretty the same with Wisdom, inside the shape of way that it serves an important characteristic for the relaxation of the virtues, however furthermore as it lays the idea as for the relaxation of the virtues to behave. What is supposed via manner of that is that, if Wisdom is the how of the virtues then Temperance is the wherein and even as of virtues.

Marcus Aurelius stated in his Meditations that:

"If you are searching out tranquility, do an awful lot much less.' Or (more successfully) do what's crucial—what the logos of a social being requires, and within the requisite manner. Which brings a double delight: to do much less, better. Because maximum of what we are saying and do isn't vital. If you could eliminate it, you'll have more time, and extra tranquillity. Ask your self at each second, 'Is this crucial?'"

A lot of humans generally have a tendency to criticize this shape of declaration due to how horrible it could be. Is it a proposal for us to dispose of the things in existence that supply us hardships? Is it suggesting that we live for a good deal an awful lot less and obtain tranquility within the much less? Or is it about searching out happiness in the less?

All of the questions said above are incorrect, however legitimate. Most of the time, we people will be inclined to appearance having lots much less as essentially the equivalent of being unsuccessful, which then comes complete circle end sooner or later comes decrease once more to the amount concept that ends in the notion of being bad. For the human psyche that has been informed thinking about that our days in pre-college that stars is higher than one huge call, accepting the kind of concept may be drastic, if now not not viable. But such is the training of the Stoics.

What Aurelius is really asking us proper right here isn't to surrender matters in our existence, but to give up baggage that soak up vicinity in our day by day thoughts. Although this can also be completed in pretty some techniques in its physical, quantitative, maximum price effective, and environmental factors, Aurelius posits that thru decongesting our luggage, we become greater enlightened or 'tranquil' sufficient to look what's in reality crucial.

He is not asking us to pick out and choose out what to eliminate from our lives. He is calling us to sell off or allow bypass. The distinction in removing from unloading or letting move, is that the previous way deletion or eradication, whilst the latter way to be unburdened or to be eased. By looking at it in this way, we now see that the riding motion that is despite the fact that needed to exercise this one of a kind function is control.

You must understand that you can allow circulate. That's authentic temperance. It is not in casting off the unessential, however it's miles allowing yourself to permit skip. It is understanding that once in a while, you may allow bypass of things which is probably from your manipulate. By doing so, you presently create a roadmap for the rest of the virtues to behave upon and make an effect in your lifestyles.

Wisdom now has an much much less complicated challenge as it's far complimented inside the locating of power for manage given with the resource of Temperance. Wisdom now most effective has to decide how a great deal control you are both inclined to give up for a said mission or how lots strength you will set up to make a purpose truth. Justice and Courage may additionally revel in the roadmap because it will inform them in which to place nice selections or emotions whilst handling great humans, stressful conditions, or aspirations in life. Practical Application

Now, to use Temperance as a exercise for your each day existence is difficult, but clean. Again, it's miles great in case you start off small in advance than growing into the bigger elements that surround you. You can start education Temperance via genuinely deciding on to allow pass of conduct. Whatever addiction you could choose out, it does now not depend. What your motive is supposed to be, is to understand and make your self familiar with the feeling of letting go with the flow.

Let's say the dependancy you're letting pass of is your dependancy of waking up late. Now what you need to do is check why you're letting skip of it first. You endure in thoughts instances it has pressured you. Now you decide to softly and regularly allow this form of dependancy go with the resource of appreciating the benefit and the lightened load you're slowly having. A sensible end end result of that is the gradual but great interest that thru letting bypass of waking up late, you currently permit your self a far more lenient time desk on the same time as warding off to each school or art work. Thus, a exquisite act or problem of your life will become a good buy lots plenty an lousy lot much less burdened and is therefore, come what may additionally moreover moreover, tranquil. This is the maximum minimum however sensible way of questioning and the use of temperance on your each day life. The gist proper right here is which you permit go along with the glide because of the reality you can.

In totality, every Wisdom and Temperance gas the life of a Stoic. It drives you to carry out better, supply lesser, and be wiser. At this problem, you may think which you determined the entire of those standards but one need to no longer count on that, another time, those will no longer be of gain to you without a doubt if not finished alongside detail the rest of the virtues. Namely, Courage and Justice.

## Chapter 9: Justice and Courage

The worldwide nowadays is in need of justice. Because of this, courage, as we recognize it, has risen exponentially as moves from splendid people and races rise up and communicate to for alternate worldwide. But what's justice? What is braveness?

The idea of justice that has been current at a few degree inside the region has been approximately how those who had performed incorrect be treated with the proper punishment. Justice has extended been associated with thoughts collectively with the hand or the hammer. Such descriptions and thoughts of justice has been the fuel for optimum of what has been taking area spherical the location, this is injustice.

When we have a take a look at justice as this determine of power and of destruction, then it's miles natural for people to influence smooth of and get out of its manner. Don't get me wrong, people who have done incorrect ought to be handled the right sanctions and reformation techniques for them as a manner to return to society as well functioning humans. The element right proper proper right here is, justice does now not want to be understood so strictly or so destructively.

There is a cause why justice is symbolized via way of the use of the use of a lady who holds a scale and is blindfolded. Not quality does this endorse that there should be no bias, because of the blindfold, however furthermore for there to be a balance. The scale represents such balance. To create stability, the burden on each scales should be same. Here, we are delivered to a concept we're now so acquainted with, however missing. Equality.

The truth is justice cannot do what it is meant to do, if there can be no equality. If justice proceeds with a scale this is slightly unbalanced, then there need to be a wrongdoing to purpose such. The equality being said right proper proper right here does not suggest the equality of what is being weighed, for the cause that this act relates to the trialing itself. But instead refers to the dimensions itself.

Its scales want to be in same stability for it to art work the manner it have end up supposed to art work. How may additionally want to you experience if you went to the marketplace and purchased gadgets from a dealer who has a broken scale, and therefore growing the fee of this properly that you had offered? The identical goes for justice. Nothing will skip the proper manner it is meant to, if from the start, the scales have already been tipped.

On the possibility hand, courage has in no way been on display as lots as it's miles now. Courage is proper right right here and it's miles fanning the flames of each person's hopes and goals. Courage has normally been there in us. The hassle is someplace alongside the road people decided on to be comfortable. Now, there can be no longer a few factor wrong with being in a snug characteristic. That's an entire wonderful ball interest of concept there.

Comfort, as it's far being framed proper proper proper right here, isn't a rustic however a choice. It isn't a noun however is as an possibility a verb. Comfort has been sealing in our feelings, our reactions, our desires, and our need for trade in our lives. The purpose in which one-of-a-type human beings don't advantage lifestyles isn't due to the fact they're now not snug with in which they may be now, but as an opportunity they decided straight away to be snug with wherein they will be from the very starting. The preference to be comfortable is a preference of costly given to those who accumulate achievement, or to those who've lengthy past through the demanding conditions needed to have the ability gain such consolation.

Now, in case you are any person who has no longer but built a map, at least, of the way to accumulate your desires and then making a decision to be cushty, then courage moreover includes a choice to be comfortable. What is taking place inside the worldwide nowadays, is that human beings are in the long run waking as lots as this faux concept of comfort that they'd made for themselves. When tragedy, crime, and calamity movements and so near us, repetitively, then the veil of comfort is torn. Courage is now over again at the motive strain's seat. Courage starts offevolved offevolved offevolved offevolved with this. Courage starts offevolved offevolved offevolved with resisting comfort.

Marcus Aurelius wrote in his Meditations:

"And a strength of will to justice for your private acts. Which method: concept and motion ensuing inside the not unusual real. What you've got got had been given been born to do."

Marcus stated this due to the truth for him, justice became the maximum critical virtue of all, which made enjoy due to the reality the character held power. For the Stoics, they hold justice at a better large that we apprehend it these days from a jail thoughts-set.

The Stoics undergo in mind that justice is the final contact of all virtues, as it bonded and made certain society works. If there can be no justice, then society is failing. In Cicero's De Officis, he described justice with six principles. First is that no person need to case harm to each special. Pretty self-explanatory, to be honest. Second is that one treats not unusual possessions as commonplace possessions, and personal possessions as non-public.

What he intended via this is the way we behavior usage. The usage of private possessions is absolutely as a first rate deal because of the fact the proprietor, however for using common possessions, the utilization need to be determined as to what is beneficial and agreeable for all who use the shape of possession.

Third is that we ought to apprehend that we are not born for ourselves on my own. It is actual, we aren't born for ourselves by myself. We are also born for the sector we stay in, to cultivate it and make it livable. We furthermore stay for others, who feature our own family and pals.

Fourth is the idea that guy is introduced to lifestyles for the sake of diverse guys and for the sake that they do top to each tremendous. This can be very much like the preceding idea and should additionally be understood likewise. Fifth is how he prescribes that we use nature as a guide to make a contribution our element to the not unusual appropriate. Not high-quality does this endorse nature, as in what is round is, however moreover the person of our being. By considering such, we turn out to be more knowledgeable as to how we cope with each high-quality. Lastly is that Cicero described justice as high-quality religion, steadfastness and fact.

Now the question arises. How are we able to exercise the ones massive requirements of justice to our lives? Before that, to actually understand what justice is, we want to furthermore highlight what it isn't always. For the Stoic, it is pretty smooth but difficult to recognize. For them, injustice, or what is not justice, is to motive damage or damage to each distinct being. Again, smooth however hard to recognize and exercise for maximum people. The cause inside the once more of such trouble is because of the truth the Stoics outline it as to reason and no longer to injure or to harm. This manner we want to be privy to our movements thinking about we in no manner recognize what it may do to others. Here, we flow into lower back to the concept of Wisdom and the same antique of manage we need to uphold.

Practical Application

Now, to exercising Stoic justice almost in our lives, we want to start somewhere small. Again, the idea is to start small for the very cause that we may be capable of workout introducing change in a controlled way and in a no longer so drastic scale.

Stoicism shows that we begin first through reforming our mind of others indoors ourselves. What this indicates is, in advance than searching out to be impactful and deal with everybody with equity, we want to first trade our mindsets about who and what distinct human beings constitute in our lives. There ought to be a reexamination first, in advance than the actual exercise.

That being said, be aware of all the humans to your life. Catalogue them and take a look at your treatment for anybody. Look decrease decrease lower returned at your reviews in handling those one-of-a-kind styles of people. Understand the topics you have got had been given have been given completed wrong and attempt to frequently change your perception of them which have been the reason of you doing them wrong.

This needs to seem in advance than we exit and ask forgiveness for the people we've got were given wronged. If you skip this and keep to ask forgiveness really due to the fact you want to elevate that weight off your shoulder, you then virtually are simplest certain to do such an act with a one-of-a-kind man or woman. The purpose why that is prescribed is because of the reality how can everyone be identical at the same time as our belief of numerous human beings is already disjointed and biased? Justice's notable evidence is equality. And equality can exquisite be accomplished if we change our perceptions, our practices, our conduct, our notions, our suggestions, our criminal tips, and our biased truths approximately precise people.

As Epictetus had written in his Discourses:

"Don't existence is type of a military advertising and marketing and advertising marketing and advertising advertising and marketing and advertising and marketing advertising campaign? One want to serve on watch, each distinct in reconnaissance, each other at the the front line... So it's miles for us—anyone's existence is a form of warfare, and an extended and varied one too. You need to hold watch like a soldier and do the whole thing commanded... You had been stationed in a key located up, no longer a few lowly region, and now not for a fast time however for life."

What Epictetus is trying to say right right right right here is that we have to all attempt to be on guard. Another quote with the beneficial resource of Epictetus that might once more up this declaration is while he stated that: "Two terms ought to be dedicated to memory and obeyed, persist and face up to." The cause in the decrease again of this is that braveness is perfectly displayed, in step with Stoics, on the identical time as we resist and persist the topics that take control or select out to damage our lives or the lives of others round us.

What the Stoics imply thru the usage of this is not to get up to and outright act recklessly, which could in the long run bring about the damage of others. For a Stoic to face up to and persist, it also manner to manipulate feelings and keep them in test surely so we emerge as more green in acting the rest of the virtues being required of a Stoic. Yet this doesn't suggest that a Stoic is a person who is passive.

Considering all the virtues that have been mentioned, a Stoic is a person who is absolutely active in insisting a higher life for others and in promoting the truth. The extremely good distinction a Stoic has from a senseless man shouting his truths, is that a Stoic is able to maintain the whole thing in check and is in a characteristic to talk truths not high-quality critical to him however furthermore truths vital to others spherical him, in a way wherein no purpose to damage or injure is started out out.

Seneca have end up one who is a top instance of this. Facing lack of life on the hands of a tyrant he had been a mentor of, the character said: "Nero can kill me, but he can not damage me." Such is the composure of someone who has been meditating and placing his time into the development of courage. A courage informed with information, temperance, and mainly, justice.

Marcus Aurelius moreover had a danger to exhibit his braveness at the equal time as he have grow to be being tested thru using way of way of using a failing and decomposing Roman Empire. At a time at the equal time as nearly each valid is corrupted and seeking out to higher their very non-public lives before setting the lives of the people they serve first, Marcus Aurelius stood steadfast and relied no longer super on himself but furthermore the humans near him to offer all over again what he has been giving them from the very beginning, this is understanding, temperance, justice, and courage. Courage, to sum up, works nicely with the opportunity virtues because it lovers the flames for them. Courage allows those virtues to behave and to sincerely waft and take movement closer to the subjects we, and Stoics, have set their dreams on.

Practical Application

To exercising braveness almost in our every day lives, one most effective has to have a have a check the subjects which are constantly difficult us on a each day foundation. When we're coping with such disturbing situations in our lives, whether or not or no longer or no longer or now not or no longer impacting an entire network socially and ideologically, or going thru our very very own demons, the awesome manner to workout courage is to clearly rise up on the same time as we are knocked down via way of these traumatic conditions.

Again, from an software utility software software thoughts-set, it is straightforward however difficult. In mild of the troubles we're going via nowadays, braveness, regardless of the fact that sufficient, is likewise on the identical time in want of refreshment. If we've got a have a have a look at the individuals who are beginning and continuing actions global, earlier than focusing an excessive amount of on how loud their cries are, permit's try to study what we're able to deliver them to lighten the load on their shoulders.

Courage surely is not about doing extravagant topics on this problem in time, as we are constrained in our interactions, but is ready deciding on to rise up and to upward thrust up off our snug positions in lifestyles and decide to impact trade everywhere it desires to be seen.

Before concluding this monetary disaster, it need to be said yet again that none of these virtues can also want to art work on their very very very non-public on the same time as practiced. There need to be a regular devotion in the route of the betterment of oneself, as a manner to completely be able to draw close to and manage the virtues which may be crucial to a Stoic.

Now, in advance than intending to the following financial catastrophe, it's miles cautioned that the reader assessment the four virtues earlier than tackling the three disciplines of Stoicism, featured within the next economic wreck. Since pretty some confusion may additionally furthermore furthermore take place even as expertise what differs the groups of ideologies and their programs in each day life.

## Chapter 10: The Three Disciplines of Stoicism

After discussing the 4 virtues of Stoicism: information, temperance, courage, and justice; we now keep to the 3 disciplines. The said disciplines are none apart from: Desire, Action, and Assent. Here is a quote from Epictetus that talks approximately the importance of the stated disciplines:

"There are three departments in which someone who's to be suitable and noble need to benefit information of. The first issues the want to get and will to keep away from; he should take a look at not to fail to get what he wills to get nor fall into what he wills to avoid. The 2d is concerned with impulse to behave and not to behave, and, in a phrase, the sphere of what's becoming: that we need to act so as, with due interest, and with right care. The item of the zero.33 is that we won't be deceived, and may not decide at random, and typically it is worried with ascent." In clean phrases, Desire is to be understood as Stoic Acceptance, Action to be Stoic Philanthropy, at the identical time as Assent as Stoic Mindfulness.

But earlier than we maintain into discussing each of the disciplines, it need to be first understood that they range from the virtues on this type of way that the virtues are the soul at the identical time because the disciplines characteristic the frame. The disciplines are the walking tool for the packages which can be the virtues. These have to no longer be pressured with the opportunity.

The Discipline of Desire

The region of Desire enacts to reveal us what our goals or dreams should be, it honestly is pushing in the course of desires or topics which can be in our manage. This region is carefully related to the virtues of Courage and Temperance. The motive in the back of it's far because of the fact Courage can help Desire to push closer to a purpose, at the equal time as Temperance distinguishes whether or now not or not or no longer or now not purpose is pursuable or no longer.

When looking at how a Stoic guy desires to stay his existence, this is the terrific proof of his Stoicism. This is because of the reality the world of preference is ready pushing nearer to finish popularity of what it is to control the final results of a reason. Although no longer the direct software of the Stoic necessities, this area allows the undertaking which does so.

Desire is also referred to as Stoic Acceptance. Now, on the same time as you consider it first, why beauty of all topics? If you placed the phrases thing with the useful beneficial aid of element: Desire and Acceptance; it seems that they have no applicable connection the least bit to every unique. But if we have got a test it from a Stoic mind-set, the reason in the decrease returned of such is because of the fact the Desire of a Stoic guy ought to be shrouded in Acceptance. Acceptance lets in us to recognize. Acceptance gives us peace.

Acceptance reevaluates our dreams and elements us to goals which is probably better becoming for us, which we also can manipulate.

Acceptance prevents unhappiness brought about via using the usage of uncertainty, thru permitting us to stay a existence wherein we slowly convey together the steps inside the direction of our goals and not gather our dreams beforehand of our steps. Acceptance is the know-how that topics do take time and that we're to be affected individual with that issue.

A top instance of Desire as Stoic Acceptance is in how someone builds the stairs earlier than trekking them. If someone have been to construct a cause or a immoderate shape first, earlier than building the stairs to achieve such, he's going to continuously fall and damage himself as he has no useful aid in building inside the course of this excessive reason. And with the useful aid of the save you of it, if he ever finishes it, he may additionally moreover have nowhere else to transport however down. And recall you me, he is going to feel possibly harm greater than the excessive he felt at the identical time as he "finished" his purpose. But if someone slowly builds his way in the direction of an present day goal, some thing this is rational and already there, his adventure will become fuller of certainties in area of uncertainties.

He starts offevolved offevolved offevolved via building small steps. Making tremendous each step is powerful and able to hold his weight whilst he eventually makes a desire to climb the mountain that is his cause. He then pushes towards constructing slightly higher steps. He may additionally additionally fall now and again, however it's far no longer some aspect surprising because of the truth he is looking down within the course of the stairs he is constructing, in region of the height he's aiming to attain.

Through this slow but awesome manner, the character is able to gain a motive he has been wishing to gain for good-bye, through a managed way and way wherein manipulate at the helm of everything else. The motive within the over again of as to why manipulate come to be capable of take manipulate of the helm of this man's approach is because of the reality Acceptance gave it to him. He big the assignment that have turn out to be earlier.

He favored that it have end up a top he couldn't gain thru locating out the limits of uncertainty. He ordinary that he can be disappointed along the manner as mistakes is a natural a part of existence. And most significantly, he commonplace that the first rate manner he is to climb that top, is with the useful aid of approach of creating or controlling in fact the steps he's taking and placing aside the stairs he couldn't, may also additionally need to have, and must no longer take.

If he spent his time meandering and brooding about, he would possibly in all likelihood have in no way reached his purpose. If he spent his time speeding and making brash alternatives, he could likely have in no manner reached his purpose. If he spent his time thinking about the steps he have to take or the shortcuts he might in all likelihood in all likelihood take, he also can moreover want to have in no manner reached his reason. Desire or Stoic Acceptance is in no way approximately what lies on the stop, however as an alternative gives primacy to what can be finished to accumulate what is at the surrender. With the spirit of Acceptance inside the again of this form of purpose, Desire then turns into a controlled emotion able to growing rational options which may be excessive awesome to help and collect the road within the path of the dreams of a Stoic guy.

Practical Application

Some realistic techniques of the usage of this for your personal life is thru way of placing goals for your self. Start with one aim first. It is normally encouraged that this number one goal, be a motive this is small in nature as you need to exercising this example grade by grade and slowly.

When setting a intention, make certain which you have a take a look at the boundaries of what you're capable of do nearly approximately that purpose. Say for example, your reason is to build up a garden to your outdoor. To do that you need to first have Courage to take on the undertaking of this sort of venture. Understand that there might be screw ups along the way and that it need to not deter you.

Then test developing a roadmap or calendar of at the equal time as you can do extremely good steps to constructing a lawn. This is wherein Temperance is available in as you can need to check the assets you cannot and might do. Then you begin to slowly bring together your garden. Sure, now and again you may face issues in the shape of damaged pipes, unwanted creepy crawlers, or damaged device; however all of that is beside the thing now due to the fact you're walking with a Stoic Acceptance it truly is

Desire. Sooner or later you may be in a feature to complete your lawn.

At this aspect, you want to reflect and look at what it took as a manner to advantage this form of motive. Notice which you are a person now who's on top of things. You have been capable of exercising control through Desire or Stoic Acceptance with the help of every Courage and Temperance. What topics in this example is that you were capable of take manipulate of the method. You have been able to enjoy the adventure that you had made for yourself. You recognise what to do and what to choose up. You apprehend that you could fail and that you may screw a few unknown stuff up.

You will maximum likely aggravate your self alongside the manner. But all of this is good sufficient due to the reality it is no longer some element that you yourself had no longer anticipated. That is Desire or Stoic Acceptance. By Temperance you recognize that a few subjects are out of your manage and via way of Courage you act upon the topics you can control.

## The Discipline of Action

Now, we go with the drift proper away to Stoic Philanthropy or Action. The Discipline of Action isn't always what it usually manner earlier than the whole thing sight. For maximum human beings, movement approach to act, to make some problem, to move, or to alternate a few aspect. For a Stoic, Action technique the actual utility of dwelling. Action, due to the fact the Stoic Philanthropy, is referred to as a topic this is more involved with what's interior.

In the equal enjoy, Action is maximum carefully related with the distinct feature of Justice. Justice is the different feature that emphasizes fairness and equality as key additives inside the way we want to address others. The purpose why the 2 are associated is because of the truth Action or Stoic Philanthropy way to be an area that strives for the welfare of others through enacting Justice. And this enacting of Justice is knowledgeable via records what is right, horrible, and detached.

The purpose behind understanding what is proper, lousy, and indifferent, isn't because of the truth so you also can need to smooth out your interactions with excessive extraordinary human beings but instead understand what's inside the lower back of clearly without a doubt anybody you meet. What this indicates, as Marcus Aurelius locations it, is that we need on the manner to empathize and recognize that the people that surround us whether or no longer or not in a superb, terrible, or indifferent manner, are all trouble to factors and defects due to the fact they themselves don't understand the splendid, terrible, and indifferent.

Aurelius, in his announcement from Meditations, calls upon us who have appeared actual, seen awful, and understood the man or woman of human beings as one, to be thoughtful and not be angered with the useful aid of any of these humans that we come upon.

Another detail of Action or Stoic Philanthropy which moves in detail with being considerate with splendid people, correct or horrible, is how as a Stoic one want to need Eudaimonia for others as properly. It is that this lively movement that runs the course of the real software program program of Action in our lives.

To refresh your memory, Eudaimonia is the Stoic's idea of very outstanding happiness or satisfaction. In this wishing and appearing of Eudaimonia for others, we need to take have a have a look at that our perception of others need to no longer be constrained. In Stoicism, only manage can be constrained however no longer the idea of giving happiness. This is because of the fact in some times, people normally usually commonly will be predisposed to disregard one of a kind people due to the truth they have got already set of their head who the others of their lives are.

When the superb Stoics talk approximately others, this indicates all. So, while you appearance to need Eudaimonia for others, be cautious now not to damage others as properly in the method. Eudaimonia want to be for all. Another detail of wishing happiness for others, is the limits of our capability within the direction of giving it. One want to continuously understand that specific human beings's happiness is outside of our talents. Although we are able to do acts that can motive their happiness, it isn't internal our gift abilities so that you can straight away effect each different's happiness.

This is in which Action or Stoic Philanthropy takes a flip yet again into its passive nature. When wishing every different individual happiness, there need to be determined a experience of detachment. By this, Stoics otherwise you who desires happiness to others can do such without detrimental yourself. Most parents which is probably within the industries of servicing notable human beings lose their power and become upset on the equal time as they'll be now not capable of help one-of-a-type humans. This want to now not be the case as it's miles in the end, genuinely as loads because of the truth the individual him/herself whether or now not or not he/she can be able to decide to be happy given the activities that he is in.

No tremendous commercial enterprise organisation of human beings top notch is familiar with the idea of Action or Stoic Philanthropy more than mother and father. Parents are pressured to understand, whether or no longer or now not or no longer or no longer or not they determine on it or now not, that they'll have no have an effect on on their infant's happiness at a exceptional aspect in time. This isn't always to mention all dad and mom are extraordinary, as a few or maximum do fall quick of such realizations. But the greater essence of being a determine is knowing that our number one interest is to nurture the environment of our kids for them to expand within the equal nurturing style as nicely.

It must be said that in this device parents moreover come to understand that there may be times in which their kids will hit rock bottom. Such unhappiness is predicted due to the fact, as dad and mom, those human beings have prolonged prolonged beyond thru the equal struggles their kids are set to experience. In this way they end up excessive examples of what it method to enact the vicinity of Action or Stoic Philanthropy. They each recognize the errors their youngsters make, and take to coronary coronary coronary coronary heart that the happiness of their children will sooner or later now not be counting on them because it have turn out to be earlier than. Practical Application

In terms of software application of Stoic Philanthropy or the area of Action toward your personal lifestyles, it is fairly simple but tough as nicely. Start with a small group of people. Now this contradicts the earlier statement of wishing happiness for all, however for the sake of training it and mastering it, such need to be considered in the intervening time. With that out of the way, select a hard and fast of human beings whom you need to start exercise this place. It may be your circle of relatives, your buddies, your co-human beings, or even your close by sports teammates.

The critical element proper proper right here is which you limit it first, for you as a way to slowly and lightly exercising the issue. You have to begin via the usage of way of being nicer to them in elegant. Give them presents, brighten their day together together together with your jokes, or truely really offer time to pay attention to them within the occasion that they need to talk. Then, if there are times while you're being each indignant or damage thru their movements, try to apprehend them. By understand, this suggests to find out wherein they will be coming from.

Understand if they'll be issue to horrible, specific, or indifferent emotions, and what is going to be inflicting such feelings to sprout out of them. That's basically it. If you're having trouble know-how them, skip returned and compare the standards of Justice and Courage. For this specific example, exercise Justice by means of way of knowing that these humans you're being angry with the aid of at instances, are just like you. They aren't any brilliant. Neither better nor lower in price than you.

Exercising the area of Action or Stoic Philanthropy is hard. Most fail but this is beside the component. Those who fail in it understand that such is life and there are matters which may be out of our manipulate. But we have to have a look at that notwithstanding such screw ups in dealing with one-of-a-kind people, we want to now not prevent in striving for engaging in Eudaimonia for all.

The Discipline of Assent

Lastly, we've got the concern of Assent or what is also referred to as Stoic Mindfulness. Assent or Stoic Mindfulness is probably the maximum non-public out of all the disciplines that have been noted. The motive for such is due to the fact this has extra to do with how our mind operates. Stoic Mindfulness problems itself with the different feature of Wisdom. This is due to the fact to practice Stoic Mindfulness, one desires in order to degree and hold take a look at of their moves, judgements, and perceptions.

If you keep in mind, Wisdom has loads do with how a Stoic thinks or assesses. Thus, the very nature of Stoic Mindfulness lies in our data of our emotions, epistemology, and psychology. Out of all the disciplines, that is the maximum important thinking about the other disciplines are wonderful to be suffering from this. Think of your thoughts as a manufacturing unit. Now this production facility is not like a few other, because of the truth in desire to being positive what substances it makes use of and what products it produces, it as an alternative bases its production from what surrounds it.

If it's miles surrounded through way of the usage of anger, then it produces some thing that has anger or is fueled with the aid of anger. If it's miles surrounded via way of worry, then it produces some aspect that has fear or is fueled through way of way of worry. If it is surrounded through love, then it produces some thing that has love or is fueled via love. Epictetus teaches us to preserve this production facility in check. To positioned up walls and control what comes outside and inside. To articulate what's being used and produced.

He goals us to have a judgement, moves, and perceptions which may be examined. The figuring out factor of what's to be had in and what comes out on the identical time as we bring together a wall, falls under the arms of the unique function this is Wisdom. Wisdom courses and continues a test and balance of these emotions. The outcome or fruit of this check and balance is that our decisions, our movements, our reactions, and our feelings are understood inside the kind of lever in which we aren't amazed or dissatisfied with the turnout of the activities in our lifestyles.

This nearly way that once we enjoy that we are unhappy, we routinely pinpoint why so thru the assessments and stability that Wisdom has finished for us. This does now not constantly endorse that the wall is pretty of a dictatorial assemble. It remains truly as an entire lot as you what you positioned indoors your brain and what comes out of it. Wisdom is surely there to manual you and help you. It does not typically imply that our thoughts want to most effective invite in proper and deflect some thing horrible.

If such is the case, then it'd be disastrous if a few element horrible slips in with out our have a study. The university of our mind can be careworn out as it has not been used to feeling some trouble horrible. In Stoic

Mindfulness or Assent, it does not depend if the idea is good or horrible. What subjects is that there may be Wisdom to hold a take a look at and balance on our mind. So that on the surrender of the day, we aren't amazed or taken aback with the useful resource of emotions, picks, and movements that pop out humans. Being properly knowledgeable through this system of check and stability moreover manner that we are able to discover ways to method those high-quality emotions, judgments, and moves in a higher fashion so they serve the other disciplines well sufficient.

Practical Application

The pleasant manner to apply this in your existence is with the useful resource of looking inward all the time and growing a diary of some sort of the emotions that had you undergo on a each day basis. You don't constantly want to shape a wall already to your mind at the same time as you're surely beginning out to exercise this Stoic place. Start by using the use of monitoring what comes out of you and then flow on into tracing as to in which need to that emotion, judgement, or motion, probably can also need to have come from.

It is best after constantly strolling closer to this region that you can start to construct a wall spherical the schools of the thoughts so that you can be capable of then see for your self what is going into your thoughts and in a while controlling or informing yourself of the reasons on why such an movement came out of you. Once greater, that is pretty easy but very tough. But with pretty a few persistence and acknowledgement, such manage over the schools of the mind can be performed.

Before this bankruptcy ends, we must first recap the three disciplines and apprehend in which the Stoics have derived them from. This is vital as it permits us apprehend the disciplines on a more theoretical degree.

For Desire or Stoic Acceptance, it is been derived from Physics. The motive is because Acceptance is tied with records the topics we're capable of or can't manipulate, which in flip may be understood due to the fact the laws of this global or as scientists like to name them, Physics. For Action or Stoic Philanthropy, it changed into derived from Ethics. This is pretty self-explanatory given that each the problem and the concept of Ethics deal with how we behave round or for the opposite. Lastly is the Stoic Mindfulness or Assent. This field come to be derived from Logic, because it makes use of the concept of motive in tracing, knowledge, and filtering the bits and bobs of our thoughts.

## Chapter 11: Applying Stoicism in Your Daily Life

The implementation or software application of Stoicism itself for your each day lifestyles is best possible if you continuously immerse in Stoic teachings. In this financial damage, prescriptions is probably given as to the way to nearly immerse and exercise the Stoic teachings that were noted earlier. Something to take word in advance than persevering with is which you want to continually apprehend that much like anything else, schooling Stoicism takes time. It can also even come to instances in which you're dubious if it will ever be simply right for you. That's remarkable. It is best natural for us to suppose on this shape of manner. But recognize as properly, that no person turns into a maintain near at some thing on his first try. Things take time.

Throughout this economic destroy, there may be references to the four virtues and the three disciplines as this moreover serves as a little by little application or recap of the aforementioned thoughts.

Read More

This method that you have to well known that your records remains lacking, if this is your first come across with Stoicism. If now not, then it without a doubt ought to not harm to comb up on what has been taught and what's continuingly being superior within the philosophy. It isn't always possible for one to virtually without delay come to be a Stoic after analyzing this e-book. The steps and examples written right here are virtually tiny snippets into feeling out the system of being a Stoic or utilizing its requirements in your lifestyles.

Not simplest does reading extra will can help you find out a plethora of information on the assignment, however moreover continuously remind you of what you are trying to look at or exercise. Such is Stoicism. If we are to shield our minds and ultimately form a wall spherical, which we name Assent or Stoic Mindfulness, then we might need regular reminders and blueprints inside the shape of numerous

Stoic teachings. Wisdom does not pop out of nowhere, it's far instead advanced through constant revel in and gaining knowledge of. Take study that this step or tool is a persevering with one, and should not prevent.

Take Control

Another step that must be taken to properly put into effect Stoicism on your every day lifestyles is with the beneficial aid of operating out your inner or emotional control. To try this, you have to take note of the virtues of Temperance, Wisdom, and the sector of Assent or Stoic Mindfulness. The cause in the back of such is because of the reality the stated necessities are considerable to the idea of emotion and manipulate.

These days, we're continuously bombarded with the useful resource of information that push you nearer and in the direction of the threshold until you ultimately snap and abandon all control. It is vital that during case you are to workout Stoicism in recent times, as relevant and properly timed as it is able to be, you must take be aware of those issues and difficulties that such an commercial enterprise enterprise faces. It won't be clean. Especially now that our identities are cramped collectively within the ever-converting worldwide of the internet.

One realistic manner of developing this inner manage is through distancing from the internet for a fast time body, and allowing handiest quick scheduled peeks at it. By this, you aren't simplest controlling you very own utilization of technology but additionally the consumption of emotion and noise this is inflicting you to be driven nearer and inside the direction of the threshold. Another step vital to this technique is knowing the boundaries of it slow. Understand that component is restrained. This is why you need to take a look at how you use it as regards the feelings which you absorb. This is essential as hundreds of our inner and emotional control is based on how we manipulate our time.

Know What Makes You Happy

A step that want to be taken as nicely is to check and find the supply of 1's happiness. This approach that before we choose out to be glad, allow us to first take a look at where we base this happiness from. The motive why this is so important is due to the fact quite a few our happiness stands on risky floor. And while this ground finally gives way, so will our happiness too.

Instead of unstable floor, allow us to alternatively located the concept of our happiness on sturdy ground or on someplace we ourselves had based totally. We pass decrease again now to the instance in advance of building steps at the equal time as aiming to achieve a intention, approximately the issue of Desire or Stoic Acceptance.

When building our goals or happiness, we need to base them on floor we ourselves have cultivated or have manipulate of. This is not to mention that our happiness will constantly be there, and we obtained't be disenchanted in some unspecified time in the destiny of our life. We will stumble and we're capable of fall really in this lifetime. But as Marcus Aurelius has illustrated in his quote: "Alexander the Great and his mule reason strain every died and the identical difficulty happened to every", not some thing endures.

What this shows is that everyone is a protagonist of their own reminiscences however every person can be meeting the same destiny on the give up of our lives. By meditating in this sort of reality, we expand an thoughts-set wherein we're not amazed or disappointed by using way of tragic events in our life for the cause that we are now informed of our manipulate of our existence and the reality or eventual fate of our lifestyles.

Solidify Your Resolve

The final tip or step that must be taken observe of is to keep your ground through the assist of Courage and Justice, with the Stoic discipline of Action. This manner that a few component might also come our manner, we're to be unfazed and status sturdy. This serves as a totally crucial practice in case you are to place into effect Stoicism to your existence. This might be the great proof of a person living a Stoic lifestyles. Remember how human beings feature the phrase Stoic, to someone who is unfazed and unbothered by using the issues in his or her existence? Well this is exactly what it technique to be a Stoic.

Seneca himself come to be as calm as may be whilst requested to devote suicide through the usage of his former pupil, in the front of his circle of relatives. This is not to mention that we should be impervious to the sufferings of the arena. The very reason why Courage and Justice along aspect the Stoic subject of Action is blanketed into the exercising of getting an unwavering spirit is due to the reality however those problems, a Stoic must push for the better change irrespective of what the charge.

This is why such reverence and reward is given to the extremely good Stoic sages. These guys were subjected to the severa, but most harsh conditions diagnosed to guy. Yet other than reputation their ground and being evidence against uncontrollable emotions and moves, additionally they sought to offer the betterment of the lives of their fellow men. They taught, they dominated, they mentored, and that they dedicated their time to the individuals who've been beneath them. Such is the heavy load of being a Stoic. Thus, if one had been to put into effect Stoicism through being steadfast and strong in instances of chaos, one has to additionally don't forget the processes in which he can be a contribution to the solution of the problem accessible.

You can be experiencing troubles in your life now that seem to envelop your lifestyles in darkness. You can be improving or grieving from the shortage of a loved one. Whatever struggling it could be which you're going via, apprehend which you are however on pinnacle of things of your life, not some thing endures, and that our purpose within the international is to spread happiness to all.

**Chapter 12: Living the Life of a Stoic**

Living a Stoic existence has hundreds of blessings, specifically if one is to apply it throughout those times. Here are some of the numerous blessings that consist of living a existence as a Stoic. But it need to be mentioned that if any of the standards noted in advance be eliminated or not be decided and pondered upon, then such blessings which is probably to be mentioned will now not be completely executed.

1) People's reviews matter plenty tons less to you.

It seems quite apparent to mention this at this problem however as a Stoic, this is probably one of the maximum rewarding advantages there may be. When the arena has grew to emerge as hypersensitive and a tiny mistake must earn you a whirlwind of toxic backlash, gaining knowledge of to care an entire lot a good deal much less of what particular humans anticipate serves as an oasis. But this oasis comes at a rate. The charge is to take responsibility of your self.

Having referred to the virtues and the disciplines, this have to now not come as a surprise. However, the turnout is some component just a few people in this earth genuinely revel in. You will learn how to care an lousy lot lots much less and consequently stress much less. This does no longer mean that a Stoic ignores everything this is being said of him or her. This first-rate way that you don't forget in yourself sufficient to recognize that listening to unique people's opinion approximately you and residing on it would best do you greater damage than suitable.

2) Your time will not be wasted.

Stressing an awful lot less approximately what special human beings have to mention about you, furthermore way that you may have more time for greater powerful sports. Huge components of dwelling as a Stoic is having manage and knowledge that now not whatever endures. These ideas are adapted and pondered in the virtues and disciplines. For others, the ones standards also can seem like too heavy to go through. But for a Stoic, this provides an opportunity to stay existence to the fullest and to refrain from losing time. Although a cliché, the concept of residing each day as if it's miles your final is really very reflective of Stoic teachings.

By meditating at the truth that lifestyles is fleeting, a Stoic is then able to use his or her time extra wisely and greater diligently. This also results in awareness and better exceptional in anything you may be doing. Since lifestyles is ephemeral, you may want to make your mark inside the global with the resource of giving your incredible in the whole lot that you do. Live and love to the fullest for our time in this worldwide is short.

three) We discover ways to prioritize what we are able to control

We all bring fears, frustrations, and failure. We also supply hopes, goals, and victories. Each of what we characteristic both has an similarly splendid or further horrible factor to it. We dream of getting wealthy, however get annoyed if we're nowhere close to to accomplishing it. We hope for peace and fear conflict. Our lives are filled with topics we can't control and frustrations that each one stem from legitimate and actual reasons. Yet the frustration itself, the out of control launch of emotion, for a Stoic, is never valid. Stoicism engraves it in their philosophy that we need to constantly popularity at the things we're able to manipulate and set apart the subjects we can not manipulate.

four) Distractions will depart.

Rightfully so, at the identical time as you choose to take manage of your life, you in flip allow yourself to be plenty much less susceptible to distractions. This requires a ton of reputation and control over the colleges of our mind, but it'll repay as you'll be capable of dedicate it sluggish more to the topics that rely. In a international in which it's far unusual to look a person sitting by myself simply with their mind, this serves as a lifesaver.

Most of the time, the topics we do to keep us from being bored, also are the matters that get us distracted. Playing video video video games, looking random YouTube movies, or scrolling thru your Facebook timeline are not terrible subjects themselves, but they grow to be negative whilst you permit some time be fed on by way of the use of such, with out you even noticing.

5) Anxiety will become lots tons less of a hassle.

Yes, it's miles right that within the starting of the e-book it become thoroughly sure how this shall no longer feature a highbrow fitness prescription or medicine. But within the spirit of aiming to accumulate Eudaimonia for all, Stoicism allows in lowering anxiety. By schooling Stoic teachings to your each day existence, you can often see how less and much less of your life begins to treatment as you learn how to permit move of the stuff you cannot manipulate. You turns into greater thankful however additionally forgiving of yourself.

Remember, Stoicism does not assure that there can be no more pain, however as an opportunity teaches to count on the ache in order that it hurts a whole lot a good deal much less. What we see coming won't surprise us as we already recognize in which it comes from. A pronouncing frequently said in boxing is that the punch that hurts the maximum is the best you don't see coming. Stoicism teaches us that each one punches may be visible from a mile away if we pleasant consciousness.

6) Less turns into more.

Lastly, we learn how to stay a extra content material cloth lifestyles. To a Stoic, some thing your condition may be, you already have what you need to be glad. This emphasizes how human beings evidently want to have more to keep our hype and anticipation on a excessive. But if we take a close to check our lives and put off all the regular additions, we are capable of realise that we have were given have been given greater than what we need to guide a glad lifestyles.

By deciding on less, we pick out to no longer crave and thirst for what's extra. Of direction, this is not to position to the issue the economic disaster taking place in precise nations. But basically, the essence of this advantage is to allow ourselves to take mind-set of strategies we aren't in reality "horrific" however as an opportunity bountiful in our goals. Then as a Stoic we come into the belief that more of the area goals Eudaimonia. Then we act on this to resolve the location's awesome crises.

As Seneca had famously said: "It isn't always the person who has too little but the man who craves for more, this is awful."

AMAZING STOIC QUOTES TO OVERCOME STRUGGLE & KEEP CALM DURING TOUGH TIMES & CREATE A POWERFUL MINDSET & STOIC MINDSET

Every time you want a short "injection" of electricity and steering, come to this segment straight away.

These stoic affirmations will help to maintain you calm within the path of difficult instances (this segment is divided into instructions together with: grief, happiness, achievement, procrastination, and so on.) So, each time you need a few brief steerage, virtually visit the class that maximum suits your situation in lifestyles.

Anger

"Self-manage is power. Right idea is mastery. Calmness is electricity," – James Allen

"You're higher off no longer giving the small topics extra time than they deserve." – Marcus Aurelius

"Man conquers the sector by means of the use of conquering himself." – Zeno of Citium (founder of stoicism)

"Remember, it is not sufficient to be hit or insulted to be harmed, you should accept as true with which you are being harmed. If a person succeeds in scary you, realize that your mind is complicit in the provocation. Take a second earlier than reacting, and you can find it simpler to keep manipulate." – Seneca

"You shouldn't deliver events the energy to evoke anger, for they don't care in any respect." – Marcus Aurelius

"Anger is in brief energizing, but in the end hard. Anger clouds our judgement, primary us into one disaster after some one of a kind. Anger allows all of us able to horrifying us to control our conduct. Find a gasoline that burns purifier." - @TheStoicEmperor

"You don't have to show this into some factor. It doesn't must disenchanted you." – Marcus Aurelius

Anxiety

"Many of the anxieties that harass you're superfluous, expand into an ampler place, letting your thoughts sweep over the entire universe." – Marcus Aurelius

"Concern have to strength us into motion and now not into despair. No guy is loose who can not manipulate himself" – Pythagoras

"This is an generation of ordinary hyperbole. Every day offers you a modern-day day banality disguised as an emergency. Distrust your first reactions. Begin with the idea which you are overreacting. Conserve your emotional strength in your real issues" - @TheStoicEmperor

"Instead of seeing how everything is toward you, you could select to see how the whole thing is for you. How the whole thing is precisely as it want to have been to help you increase. A shift in perspective modifications the whole lot." - @TheAncientSage

Chaos

"Many humans are watching for the hurricane to skip so that you can sail calm waters. They do not forestall to don't forget that at the equal time as they will be certainly the supply, they will moreover be the hurricane." - @TheStoicEmperor

"Turbulent times have a way of breathing new lifestyles into out of area motives. A damage want not live a destroy. It may be the foundation for renewal." – Unknown

Dealing with grievance (come to this segment whenever someone worrying situations you or your paintings).

"It in no way ceases to amaze me: every person love ourselves multiple-of-a-type people, however care more approximately their opinion than our private." – Marcus Aurelius, Meditations

"If you're ever tempted to search for outside approval, understand you have got were given compromised your integrity. If you need a witness, be your very private." – Epictetus

"Self-complaint is efficient and healthy. Self-loathing is neurotic and damaging. Don`t mistake one for the alternative." - Unknown

"Those who are capable of see past the shadows and lies of their way of life will in no manner be understood, let alone believed thru the loads." – Plato

"Many assume amazing success will pacify their critics. Quite the alternative. Criticism will multiply as you broaden and progress. Positive interest does now not come with out horrible interest. This is the rate of having an impact" - @TheStoicEmperor

"Why are the incredible among us often scenario to the most ruthless attacks? Many humans see a awesome example as a mirror that displays their very own failings over again at them. They must take a look at from this experience, or they will try to shatter the replicate. Many choose out the latter." - @TheStoicEmperor

"Give your self a present: the prevailing 2d. People out of posthumous reputation forget that the generations to return might be the same stressful humans they recognize now. And honestly as mortal. What does it be counted to you if they say x approximately you, or count on y?" – Marcus Aurelius, Meditations

"To stay a splendid life: We have the capacity for it. If we discover ways to be indifferent to what makes no difference." – Marcus Aurelius

"Yes, hold on degrading your self, soul. But speedy your hazard at dignity may be prolonged beyond. Everyone receives one life. Yours is nearly used up, and in preference to treating your self with understand, you have entrusted your very own happiness to the souls of others." – Marcus Aurelius, Meditations

Dealth

"Accepting the inevitable is the beginning of power and freedom." - @TheStoicEmperor

No evil is honorable: but loss of lifestyles is honorable; therefore, loss of lifestyles isn't evil. – Zeno of Citium (founding father of Stoicism)

"Death itself is a herbal incidence, it's far unavoidable, and the stoics belief that part of philosophical exercise is to get cushty with the unavoidable, reading to stand it with courage"- Massimo Pigliucci

"Death. The give up of sense-belief, of being controlled through our emotions, of mental interest, of enslavement to our our bodies." – Marcus Aurelius, Meditations

"Stop whatever you're doing for a second and ask yourself: Am I frightened of death because of the truth I received't be capable of do that anymore?" – Marcus Aurelius, Meditations Discipline

"Character is destiny." – Heraclius

"Be tolerant with others and strict with yourself." – Marcus Aurelius

"He who is not a super servant will no longer be an incredible hold close." – Plato

"Worthless human beings live best to consume and drink; human beings of well truely well worth consume and drink nice to stay." – Socrates

"Imagine for yourself someone, a version character, whose example you make a decision to comply with, in personal similarly to in public." – Epictetus.

"Good character isn't unique in in line with week or a month. It is created grade by grade, each day. Protracted and affected person attempt is needed." – Heraclitus

"I in no manner did some factor clearly worth doing via twist of destiny, nor did any of my improvements come with the resource of twist of destiny; they got here by way of labor." – Plato

"We can not live higher than in looking for to grow to be better." – Socrates

"Employ some time in enhancing yourself with the useful resource of different men`s writings, so you shall benefit with out problem what others have laboured hard for." – Socrates

"Moral excellence comes approximately because of dependancy. We turn out to be just via doing definitely acts, temperate via doing temperate acts, brave through doing courageous acts." – Aristotle

"The roots of schooling are bitter, but the fruit is ideal." – Aristotle

"No guy has the proper to be an beginner inside the count wide variety extensive type of physical training. It is a shame for someone to expand vintage with out seeing the beauty and electricity of which his frame is succesful." – Socrates

"Everywhere, at each 2d, you have the selection: to honestly take transport of this occasion with humility; to deal with this individual as he have to be handled; to approach this notion with care, so no longer whatever irrational creeps in." – Marcus Aurelius

"Repeated failure will enhance your spirit and display you with absolute clarity how subjects have to be completed." – Robert Greene

"Don`t underestimate the price of moderate attempt continually implemented." - @TheStoicEmperor

"True stoics don`t care about the very last results. They virtually care about giving their nice shot, right proper proper here, right now." - Maxime Lagacé

"A warrior must subdue himself in advance than he can subdue his enemies. Clear eyes see successfully. The quiet mind thinks calmly. The regular hand movements decisively. Mad passion flares brightly and fast burns itself out. Stoke the consistent flames of problem, statistics, and could." - @TheStoicEmperor

"A minute of rage can undo an entire life of diligent strive. Self-manage is self-protection. Most parents won't appearance returned on the moments we acted in anger

as amongst our excellent. Do now not act while the tide of rage flows in. Wait for it to go out. Then act with purpose and percent."
– Unknown

"The street to mastery is first-class traveled through folks who can tolerate being a newbie. Knowledge starts offevolved with the acknowledgement of lack of knowledge. Modern people may additionally additionally moreover want to have a take a look at and discard many abilities for the duration of their lives. Those who can embody being a amateur will thrive." - @TheStoicEmperor

"Effectiveness begins with removal. Choose your ignorances as cautiously as your pursuits." - @TheStoicEmperor

"Good making plans is coverage in competition to destiny moodiness and inconsistency. Do your crucial wondering at the same time as you're mentally sharp." - @TheStoicEmperor

"Always choice to research some component useful." – Sophocles

"If it isn't always proper, do no longer do it, if it is not authentic, do now not say it." – Marcus Aurelius

"Waste no greater time arguing what a great man ought to be. Be one." – Marcus Aurelius

"Cling tooth and nail to the following rule: now not to offer in to adversity, in no way to don't forget prosperity, and always take full word of fortune's habit of behaving just as she pleases, treating her as even though she had been really going to do the entirety it is in her energy to do. Whatever you've got were given been looking in advance to for a while comes as an lousy lot a good deal much less of a marvel."- Seneca, Letters from a Stoic

"I want to appearance what happens if I don`t give up." – Unknown

"The unexamined life is not surely well really worth dwelling." – Socrates

"Beware of the bareness of a busy life." – Socrates

"To be calm is the very quality fulfillment of the self" – Zen Proverb

Enemies

"Obsessing over your enemies will make you extra like them." – Unknown

"To experience affection for humans even though they make mistakes is uniquely human. You can do it, if you without a doubt understand: that they're human too, that they act out of loss of facts, towards their will, and which you'll each be dead in advance than lengthy. And, really, that they haven't truly harm you. They haven't diminished your capacity to select." - Marcus Aurelius, Meditations

Fear

"I am no longer asking you to be fearless. I am asking you to be brave." – Maxime Lagace

Don't allow your fears paralyze you into turning into a lesser model of yourself. Eliminate worry thru confronting what you are scared of." – David Goggins

"What absolutely frightens and dismays us isn't out of doors sports themselves, however the manner in which we recall them. It isn't always things that disturb us, but our interpretation in their significance." – Epictetus

"A stoic is someone who transforms worry into prudence, ache into transformation, errors into initiation, and preference into assignment." – Nassim Taleb

"Frightened with change? But what can exist without it? What's inside the route of nature's coronary coronary heart? Can you take a hot tub and depart the firewood because it became? Eat food with out reworking it? Can any essential machine take location with out a few element being modified? Can't you observe? It's without a doubt the identical with you — and truly as vital to nature." – Marcus Aurelius, Meditations

"Treat what you don't have as nonexistent. Look at what you've got, the assets you price most, and do not forget how lots you'd crave them in case you didn't have them. But be careful. Don't feel such pleasure which you begin to overvalue them, that it might disillusioned you to lose them." – Marcus Aurelius, Meditations

Focusing on what you may manage

"There is most effective one way to happiness and this is to stop annoying approximately topics which might be beyond the electricity of our will." – Epictetus

"Everything comes and goes in lifestyles. Happiness and sadness are brief studies that upward thrust from enjoy of perception. Heat and cold, pride and pain, will come and skip. They in no way very last for all time. So, do now not get connected to them. We don't have any manage over them." – Krishna

We need to normally be asking ourselves: "Is this some factor that is, or is not, in my manage?" - Epictetus, Enchiridion

"The stoics idea that a essential perception into human life is that a few subjects are up to us and others are not, the famous dichotomy of manage. Up to us are our choices, choices, and movements; the whole lot else is not as tons as us, due to the truth it's far stimulated with the useful resource of out of doors elements" – Massimo Pigliucci

"Embrace all chaos that is out of your manage. This is how it's miles. Why have to or no longer it is in any other case? Move the levers which is probably inside your draw close. Sharpen the blade of will. Strike with precision. Accept and undergo" - @TheStoicEmperor

"If we are able to attention on making clean what components of our day are inside our manipulate and what factors aren't, we will no longer best be happier, we can have a first-rate benefit over distinct those who fail to apprehend they're preventing an unwinnable conflict" – Ryan Holiday

"Define for me now what the 'indifferents' are. Whatever topics we can not control. Tell me the upshot. They are not something to me." - Epictetus, Enchiridion

"There is excellent strength in popularity. To completely take delivery of suffering and misfortune frees you from worry. You can understand proper times due to the reality you are not suffering from the records that they may give up (they'll). Such is the way of factors, and we have to live in accord with fact" - @TheStoicEmperor

"Control your perceptions. Direct your moves nicely. Willingly take delivery of what is outdoor your manage" – Ryan Holiday

"When you redesign your thoughts, the whole thing you enjoy is converted." – Mingyur Rinpoche

"Change is in no way painful, only your resistance to exchange is painful." – Buddhist Proverb

"Take a lyre player: he's relaxed at the same time as he performs by myself, but located him in front of an target market, and it's a one-of-a-kind story, regardless of how beautiful his voice or how properly he plays the device. Why? Because he no longer best wants to carry out well, he wants to be well received — and the latter lies outside his control."- Epictetus, Enchiridion

"It's a few issue like taking location an ocean voyage. What can I do? Pick the captain, the boat, the date, and the excellent time to sail. But then a hurricane hits… What are my alternatives? I do the simplest element I am in a feature to do, drown — but fearlessly, with out bawling or crying out to God, because I realise that what is born need to moreover die."- Epictetus, Discourses

Humility

"Set aside now after which some of days all through which you may be content with the plainest meals, and very little of it and with tough, coarse garb, and ask your self, is this what one used to dread?" – Seneca

"The secret of happiness, isn't placed in attempting to find greater, however in developing the capability to enjoy a lot less." – Socrates

"The simplest actual records is in understanding which you apprehend not whatever." – Socrates

"Until we've got started out to head without them, we fail to realize how pointless many things are. We have been using them now not because of the truth we needed them but due to the fact we had them." – Seneca

"Contentment is natural wealth. You will constantly be bad in case you preference greater, the fastest manner to riches is to do away with your greed. He who's content fabric with the least is likewise the richest. Try remembering this on the same time as you get your self down in looking a few component you don`t have." – Socrates

Legacy

What you depart in the returned of isn't always what's engraved in stone monuments, but what is woven into the lives of others." – Pericles

"Take an super difficult check human beings's ruling precept, specially of the practical, what they run away from & what they're seeking out." – Marcus Aurelius

Living In the prevailing

"It is not possible that happiness, and yearning for what isn't always present, have to ever be united." – Epictetus

"We outline ourselves an prolonged way too often by means of way of our beyond screw ups. That`s now not you. You are this individual proper now. You are the person who has found from the ones failures." – Joe Rogan

"I can be satisfied once I reap a kingdom free of misfortune. Unlikely. Misfortune may be minimized, however in no way eliminated. Life is entire of reputedly countless problem, after which existence ends. Peace need to be positioned in the imperfect present" - @TheStoicEmperor

"Focus on the instant, now not the monsters that would or might not be up earlier." – Ryan Holiday

"Learn out of your past, don`t live in it. The beyond ought to be protected, it can not be desired away, however it also have to not be allowed to eat the future. Today is day after today`s past, don`t spend it reliving the day before today. See the countless flowering of now." - @TheStoicEmperor

"Never allow the destiny disturb you. You will meet it, when you have to, with the equal guns of purpose which nowadays arm you in opposition to the present." – Marcus Aurelius

"Don't allow your imagination be crushed via lifestyles as an entire. Don't try to picture the entirety lousy that would possibly take vicinity. Stick with the situation available, and ask, "Why is this so insufferable? Why can't I undergo it?" You'll be embarrassed to answer. Then remind your self that past and future don't have any strength over you. Only the winning—or even that can be minimized. Just mark off its limits." – Marcus Aurelius, Meditations

Procrastination

"While we're postponing, life speeds via." – Seneca

"People are frugal in guarding their personal assets; but as speedy as it includes squandering time, they're most wasteful of the only thing wherein it's far right to be stingy." – Seneca

"Let us postpone not a few issue. Let us stability existence's books every day. The person who puts the completing touches on their lifestyles each day is in no manner brief of time." – Seneca

"Even in case you're going to stay 3 thousand greater years, or ten instances that, bear in thoughts: you can not lose a few other lifestyles than the only you're dwelling now, or stay some other one than the simplest you're losing. The longest portions to similar to the shortest. The present is the same for all people; its loss is the same for absolutely everyone; and it should be clear that a quick without delay is all that is misplaced. For you may't lose both the past or the destiny; how ought to you lose what you don't have?" – Marcus Aurelius, Meditations

"Soon you'll be ashes, or bones. A mere call, at maximum — or maybe this is handiest a valid, an echo. The matters we need in life are empty, stale, and trivial. Dogs snarling at each exceptional. Quarreling kids — guffawing after which bursting into tears a second later." – Marcus Aurelius, Meditations

Success

"Pleasure in the method locations perfection inside the paintings." – Aristotle

"Do no longer paintings 8 hours for a agency then move home and not work for your private desires, you aren't worn-out, you're uninspired." - Unknown

"It is a sign of weak spot to avoid displaying signs and signs and symptoms of susceptible point." – Nassim Taleb

"The path of least resistance is a terrible teacher." – Ryan Holiday

"A healthful body, a comfortable mind, a residence complete of love. These subjects can not be supplied. They must be earned." – Naval Ravikant

"It's hard to prioritize the long time while you think you want to experience cushty in each moment." – Unknown

"What a man certainly dreams isn't always a tensionless nation but as an opportunity the striving and struggling for a few cause really worth of him." – Viktor Frankl

"The extra time you spend in your pain area, the extra your comfort place will boom." – Robin Sharma

"Rather fail with honor than prevail with the resource of fraud." – Sophocles

"Discomfort is the foreign cash of achievement." – Brooke Castillo

"Think of yourself as useless. You have lived your lifestyles. Now take what's left and stay it well." – Marcus Aurelius

"The excellent revenge isn't always to be like your enemy." – Marcus Aurelius

"Don`t expect subjects to get higher with the aid of themselves. Make your self higher and with a purpose to notably beautify the area spherical you." – Unknown

"Everyone thinks about changing the area but no individual in every of changing himself." – Leo Tolstoy

"Fate leads the inclined and drags alongside the reluctant." - Seneca, Letters from a Stoic

"If you want to begin a few aspect new, you need to first gather being a novice. Beginners may additionally additionally fail and embarrass themselves regularly, that is simplest natural. Once you understand that this is the path to improvement, you may enjoy extra comfort in starting. Don`t be afraid as that is the path you need to take to boom or even mastery." – Socrates

"Our inward strength, at the identical time because it obeys nature, reacts to activities with the useful resource of the usage of accommodating itself to what it faces - to what is feasible. It desires no precise cloth. It pursues its very very own targets as events permit; it turns barriers into gasoline. As a fireplace overwhelms what may additionally have quenched a lamp. What's thrown on pinnacle of the conflagration is absorbed, fed on thru it - and makes it burn nonetheless better." – Marcus Aurelius, Meditations

"Not to anticipate it's no longer possible due to the fact you discover it tough. But to understand that if it's humanely viable, you may do it too." – Marcus Aurelius, Meditations

"Practice surely listening to what human beings say. Do your amazing to get indoors their minds." – Marcus Aurelius, Meditations.

## Chapter 13: What is Stoicism? A Brief History

As touched upon inner the appearance, Stoicism is a school of notion relating how one want to behavior themselves in lifestyles. The exercise began out in about three hundred BC, beneath the stewardship of someone in reality called Zeno of Citium. Hailing from Cyprus, Zeno came to Athens as a tourist—in keeping with later bills he emerge as genuinely shipwrecked ashore—and in a short time hooked up one in each of the maximum important moves in Greece.

Zeno held regular gatherings within the front of the famed "Painted Stoa," which in antiquity have become basically a portico or "roofed colonnade" in which public gatherings have been frequently held.

Here Zeno and his pupils would probably speak a massive style of philosophies on existence. It became the fact that the ones devotees met inside the the front of the

Painted Stoa, that they might later grow to be called "Stoics."

Zeno and his Stoics of course had been now not the best seekers of information at the block, as Athens became at the height of its philosophical reputation on the time. Both Aristotle's Lyceum and Plato's famed Academy as an instance, had been though an critical a part of the community. Stoicism emerge as initially just a few different strand in this great tapestry of highbrow discourse.

The Stoics have been in reality one enterprise among many—and an casual one at that.

Unlike one of a kind more hooked up institutions, the Stoics have been first of all a rag tag bunch without any professional organizational shape. It changed into the power of the message that held them together however, and Zeno had received a large following among Greeks by the time of his passing.

Immediately after Zeno's lack of lifestyles a scholar of his named Cleanthes then took it upon himself to preserve at the manner of existence. Shortly thereafter, Cleanthes grow to be succeeded via some other Stoic named Chrysippus. Second to Zeno, Chrysippus is probably one of the maximum influential Stoics of the age, vigorously increasing and expounding upon the muse that Zeno had laid out.

The subsequent maximum important segment of Stoicism coincided with the upward thrust of Rome. Before the instances of Empire, Rome changed into a Republic. Republican Rome might also additionally were more democratic, however it become nonetheless a navy energy to be reckoned with, whose martial could have been often growing while Stoicism have become first being advanced in Greece. As Rome prolonged its have an impact on, many Romans have come to be an increasing number of interested in the Stoics and their ideals.

www.ingramcontent.com/pod-product-compliance
Lightning Source LLC
Chambersburg PA
CBHW050409120526
44590CB00015B/1899